Triumph Over

ADD, ADHD & Tourette Syndrome

Agi Lidle

AB PUBLICATIONS A Better Life Publications

A CAUTION TO THE READER

This book is to be read and used only as a book containing the personal opinions and experiences of the author, Agi Lidle. No statement herein shall be construed as a claim or representation in use in the diagnosis, cure, mitigation, treatment or prevention of any disease or condition. This book is not a treatment guide and should not be substituted for a clinical and/or medical evaluation. Consult with a physician if you choose to eliminate prescription drugs. Withdrawal symptoms can be very dangerous and life threatening. The constitution of the United States of America validates your God given right to choose. No responsibility is assumed on the part of the author, publishers or distributors of this book if you choose to use the information contained herein for yourself or others.

Contents

PART ONE

Real Life Stories of Triumph Over
ADD, ADHD & Tourette Syndrome

PART TWO

Triumph Over Paradigm™

PART THREE

Getting Started

PART FOUR

Lidle Café Cookbook

Sandwiches and Wraps

Salad Bar

Italian

"Brunch" Special

Desserts

Author's Introduction

This book is a treasure chest of knowledge and experience. It contains educational information, easy to follow instructions for achieving positive results and real life testimonies from mothers who have "triumphed over" attention deficit and disruptive disorders with their children.

The book begins with my personal story of triumph over Tourette syndrome. With a solid education, change in diet, self-discipline, positive conditioning and self-reinforcement, I have achieved personal and professional success, without the use of prescription drugs.

I am confident the information provided in this book will answer most of your questions and guide you on a path paved with great rewards. All of the information presented is true and factual. Much of it has been distilled from my five years of experience and research.

The programs and natural health principles discussed within these pages are compatible with traditional forms of treatment, including prescription drugs.

Acknowledgements

I would like to thank my husband, Bill, for encouraging me to continue writing my books and for contributing to this book with his wisdom. A special thank you to Michal, my best friend, for helping to edit portions of this book. Thank you Mom, for encouraging me throughout my life and instilling in me the confidence to keep going and never give up. Thank you Stephanie, Jan and Lene, for sharing your stories of triumph with the world. You are special women. Thank you to the School of Natural Healing for giving me a priceless natural health education.

PART ONE

Real Life Stories Of Triumph Over
ADD, ADHD & Tourette Syndrome

chapter 1

Agi's Personal Triumph Over Tourette Syndrome

"Life,
and the art of living it,
is not in the arrival
or departure,
but in the journey"

Life and the art of living with Tourette syndrome has been a very difficult journey. Much of my life was spent hiding the obvious fact that there was something wrong with me. On the outside, I appeared confident, outgoing and filled with "Chutzpa". On the inside, I harbored shame and embarrassment.

From time to time, I wonder what I would have been like if I didn't have Tourette syndrome. Would I have been an actress, a member of a dance troupe, or a psychologist? Would I have had more drive and ambition to do more with my life, at an early age? The answers to these questions are no longer important to me. I am who I am. I accept the things I cannot change and work hard to change the things I can.

I accept the fact that I have Tourette's and the times, when out of the blue, I blurt out the words "F... Y.." or involuntarily jerk my elbow upward, not knowing when the recipient of the blow will by my husband or the wall. Most of the time I giggle. Oh well!

Although I accept these bizarre symptoms of Tourette's, I have worked hard to control them. For that matter, I am still working hard to control them.

It's very liberating and empowering to joke light heartedly about my symptoms. No one makes fun of me anymore or laughs at me. We laugh together and have fun with it.

Recently, a woman who attended my cooking class commented, "You are so pretty and have such a great figure that you have to have something wrong with you."

I am sure she noticed the rise in my eyebrows and the look of bewilderment on my face. For a few seconds, I stared back with eyes wide open and a blank expression. All of a sudden, I got what she meant.

I took it as a compliment. She was right. I suppose my symptoms make me seem more approachable.

Suddenly, Tourette syndrome doesn't seem so bad. Most of my life I have tried to hide it and cover it up. Not any more I don't. Today I am twitching through life with confidence and eagerness to share my message of hope and inspiration.

Tourette's is no longer a painful thorn in my side. It has toughened me up and made me realize that we all have something wrong with us. Mine just happens to be obvious and on the outside.

My triumph over Tourette syndrome didn't come easily. It was an arduous journey. It seemed each time I took one step forward, life pushed me back two. The following pages will reveal a glimpse into my journey through life with Tourette syndrome.

My childhood years

Dysfunctional, with a capital "D" sums up my childhood. It also seems to sum up much of society today. How many of us really had, quote unquote "a normal childhood"? What's normal anyway? The more people I meet, the more I realize dysfunctional may be the norm.

The good news is that today we are open and willing to talk about our childhoods. Not that long ago, we wouldn't dare air our dirty laundry. We are stepping out and sharing our personal lives, abuses, diseases and syndromes, along with just about everything else. We hope to free ourselves, as well as others.

I was born in Montbeliard, France in 1958. My parents fled from communist Hungary during the 1956 revolution and started a new and free life together in France. Sounds romantic doesn't it? It was anything but romantic.

My father, Joseph Barsi, grew up never knowing his father. He was teased endlessly about it. In retaliation, he becoming violent, making his classmates think twice before teasing him again. My grandmother tried to make up for his absent father but failed. My father turned to alcohol early in life and resented his mother until the day she died. Anger ticked within him like a time bomb on the verge of explosion.

My mother, Klara, had a rebellious spirit. At nineteen years of age, she escaped her homeland with only a suitcase in hand. Waving goodbye to her parents, she ran to join the 'underground railroad'. This was the last time she would see them alive. She met my father on the train on route to France. They married shortly after their arrival and had their first child, my brother Barna. I was born a little over one year later.

The time bomb inside my father began ticking louder and faster. He stayed out all hours of the night coming home only to eat, sleep and change clothes. Naturally, my mother wouldn't stand for it, but her 5 foot 1 inch stature was no match for an almost six foot tall, mean alcoholic. Even before my brother Barna was born, my father began to physically abuse her.

My mother was convinced that life in America would be the solution to all of our problems. Even though visas were hard to come by, she persisted until we were granted them.

In 1963, we arrived in America. I was four years old and my brother was five. I remember how excited my mother was when she saw the Statue of Liberty for the first time. Sadly, her excitement soon faded, as my fathers' promise to stop abusing her failed. Not only was he physically and emotionally abusing my mother, he began to belittle Barna as well.

Children need to feel safe growing up. Their parents are supposed to keep them safe and make them feel secure. My mother did all she could to keep us safe. My father failed miserably.

My childhood memories are very sad. From as early as I can remember, my brother and I lived in fear. Never knowing what kind of mood my father would come home in and whether he would be sober or drunk.

As a result of the ongoing abuse, the fire that once burnt so strong within my mother's spirit soon waned, with only glimpses of sparks fighting to ignite. "We will be alright. Don't be afraid. He won't hurt you," she promised.

Sometimes I wonder if Tourette syndrome was a result of the abuse I witnessed during my early childhood. I remember being very young when I first felt "out of control". I could not stop shaking my head or blinking my eyes. My head felt like it had kernels of corn popping inside of it and I couldn't stop them from popping. The symptoms continued for many years, but not in a very disruptive or obvious way. Over the years, the symptoms became more obvious.

Symptoms were much milder when my father was away. The minute I heard him come home, I felt an ache in the pit of my stomach and the symptoms got worse.

For a while, my symptoms seemed to help lessen the arguing between my father and mother. There I stood, shaking my head and blinking uncontrollably. Neither one could figure out what was wrong with me. Was there something really wrong with me or was I trying to get attention to keep them from fighting?

Maybe it was a combination of both. I really couldn't control myself and yet, I was using the physical symptoms (called tics) to take the attention off of my mother and draw the attention to myself. My father even got amusement out of watching and listening to the show when I boldly spoke out against his abuse. While shaking my head and blinking my eyes, I yelled, "Anyu (mom in Hungarian) is not stupid, you are! You are stupid, stupid, stupid." I was really frightened, but I knew I had to do something.

For many years, I have tried to recall the exact moment these symptoms interfered with my attention span. One day it dawned on me. I was in the sixth grade and sitting at the kitchen table doing my homework. My father came up behind me and stood over my shoulder watching. He didn't do it in a threatening manner. He genuinely wanted to help me, but it was too late. Just being around him made me nervous.

My mother told him to leave me alone and he did. From that moment on, whenever I got nervous or sat down to concentrate on something like schoolwork, the uncontrollable urge to shake my head, blink my eyes and stick out my tongue as far as I could (a new manifestation) made it practically impossible to concentrate or focus, for any length of time.

All three of these bizarre tics had to be done in simultaneous order before I could continue. It felt like a compulsion I couldn't control. When I did them all just right, I was free to continue my work. The problem was that the tics didn't stop. Every few minutes the compulsion to do all three tics took over again. It was a constant struggle to stay focused and finish whatever I was doing. It was frustrating, physically and mentally tiring and almost impossible to do homework.

Reading was the worst because trying to keep track of each line while shaking my head, blinking and sticking out my tongue made it difficult to remember my place. I had to reread paragraphs and pages many times to understand what I was reading.

Days and weeks would go by without my father coming home. When he did, my brother and I shook with fear. Not for ourselves so much but for our mother. My most horrifying memory was in fifth grade. I was eleven years old.

We heard him coming up the steps to our apartment. My mother was mad! She rushed us into our room and closed the door. As she ran for the front door, my brother and I opened the bedroom door just enough to witness the horror. He violently began attacking her.

I ran out screaming hysterically for him to stop. My brother stayed in the room in shock. Finally, the terror that evening stopped. My mother and I ran back into the room with Barna and closed the door. All three of us huddled together, crying and shaking. The front door slammed and he was gone again.

Little did I know that horrifying evening would have so much impact on both, my brother and I. My fighting spirit burst loose the second I ran out of the room to stop my father. My brother's spirit, on the other hand, was broken. He felt helpless to do anything.

That awful day, when my brother and I watched our father attack our mother, was the time my symptoms of Tourette syndrome became worse and obvious. "Control, control," I silently commanded myself to stop. The urge to blink my eyes as fast as I could while shaking my head was becoming stronger, and more frequent. I wanted to stop, but I couldn't make myself do it.

I know my mother was concerned. She felt so sorry for me and didn't know what to do. New tics began to manifest. I couldn't keep from clearing my throat. The symptoms must have been annoying, especially when we watched television. The urge was so strong that it drove my mother and brother crazy.

One time, my mother was so frustrated that she slapped me to try to get me to stop. I didn't. To this day she still feels badly about it. I tell her not to because I don't remember it and it doesn't hurt me. My mother only slapped me twice during my entire life. The second time was in high school when I disrespected her. Even then, she only slapped me across the knees.

My father never abused me physically. The abuse I suffered was second hand. Growing up witnessing my mother get physically and emotionally abused was horrible. Watching my brother get emotionally abused tore my guts out. As a result, I developed stomach problems.

I believe my father never physically or emotionally abused me because, no matter how scared I was, I stood up to him. He also must have felt sorry for me because he knew something was wrong with me.

The dreaded visit to the doctor

My mother couldn't stand it any longer. She had to know what was wrong with me. So, she made an appointment for us to see our family doctor.

Up until that point, my symptoms were still a mystery to my family. We never discussed it because as soon as my mother or brother approached the subject, I avoided it.

The dreaded day to see the doctor came. The doctor was very nice. He first spoke with my mother alone and then asked me to come in. I remember answering only a few of his questions before he made his diagnosis.

"You have Tourette syndrome and all you have to do is take a little pill every day to help the symptoms go away", he said. This magic pill was called Haldol.

Haldol was indeed a magic pill. It made my mind disappear and go to a place I'm not sure it would ever have come back from! After taking only two doses, I told my mother the pills made me feel like I was going into a tunnel from which there was no return. In addition, it made me feel disconnected from reality.

My mother was INCREDIBLE. She immediately threw them away and didn't force me to ever take medication again. I have never taken a prescription drug for Tourette syndrome since.

My grades through grade school were pretty good. I developed the ability to manage my symptoms at school, as best I could. The biggest hurdle I struggled with in grade school was paying attention and focusing on what the teacher was saying. Not only did I have physical symptoms of Tourette syndrome, I also had physical and mental symptoms of Attention Deficit Disorder.

"Control, control" said the voice inside my head. It was like concentrating on two things at once, every waking hour of the day. Part of me was trying to function like a normal kid on the outside, while the other part of me talked non-stop to my brain. "Stop, stop it", I told myself silently, sometimes slipping and blurting it out loud. People around me would say, "Excuse me?" I would respond, "Oh nothing, I didn't say anything."

You would think I would have sat in the back of my classrooms because of Tourette syndrome. Just the opposite, I always sat in the front or second row. I wanted all of my teachers to notice me and like me. At that time in my life, I couldn't bear it if someone didn't like me or said anything mean about me. I wanted to fit in so desperately.

I'm certain teachers were more understanding and lenient with my grades because they liked me and they knew I tried hard. I was also no slouch. It took me a lot longer to finish my homework and tests during class, but I always did. My intelligence was never in question. As a matter of fact... I was pretty smart.

Early on, I learned how to see pictures in my mind to help me memorize things. It was easier than repeating words and phrases over and over to learn them. My mind was too busy trying to control symptoms of Tourette's to repeat words. Even today, when I want to memorize something, I have to visualize what I am memorizing and see it as a picture or an image.

Tests were the hardest. Not because I didn't know the material, but because it was too hard to stay in control of the physical movements (tics). The classroom was usually quiet except for my stirring. I didn't want to distract the other kids and bring attention to myself.

Looking back now, it would have been easier for me if my teachers would have let me take the tests alone, somewhere other than in class with everyone else. Although during that time in my life, the special attention might have been too embarrassing to bear. I wanted to be like my peers, not different. It could have been a positive thing or it could have been negative. I never gave the teachers a chance to give me the choice.

My mother's search, my response

After I was diagnosed with Tourette syndrome, the sparks ignited and my mother's spirit was on fire once again. She was on a mission to learn everything about Tourette there was to learn. My mother felt helpless watching me try to control the symptoms. Unfortunately, there was not much written about Tourette's in those days. Whenever she did find something, she immediately shared it with me.

Still too ashamed and embarrassed to speak about it, my response to her was, "No, I don't want to hear about it. You read about it. I don't want to know." Why couldn't I bring myself to listen to her and read the literature? Why was I ashamed to acknowledge I had Tourette syndrome?

No one else in school had Tourette syndrome. As far as I knew, my friends had normal lives with fathers who seemed really nice. None of my friends knew about the war zone in my home. I never invited my friends over to my house because I never knew when my father was coming home or if he would be drunk. I told everyone my father was a salesman and he was always away on business trips.

It was during seventh grade that I began to make up lie after lie about my life. The lies were getting out of control, I couldn't keep up with them all. I was going crazy. Not only was I trying to control Tourette's, pay attention in class and get good grades, I was trying to remember what lie I told and to whom. Still I managed WITHOUT prescription drugs!

Tourette's or no Tourette's, I was going to try out for the seventh grade "pom-pom squad." One of the happiest memories of my grade school years was making the team. The joy continued through eight-grade when I was chosen to choreograph the team's routines.

I was happy and popular, regardless of who was looking at me. Boys made fun of me in grade school but it didn't bother me that much. When it did, I laughed it off. Somehow it made them stop. Sure, it hurt on the inside, but it made them stop that much faster. I learned how to be funny, so kids would laugh with me and not at me. It worked pretty well.

Having Tourette syndrome gave me compassion for the other kids who were made fun of and labeled "outcasts". I made a special effort to be their friend. If a classmate was very shy and she was eating lunch by herself, I sat down next to her or invited her to eat with my friends and I.

Even though I seemed happy on the outside (and I was most of the time at school) I was a very scared and a hurt little girl on the inside. Feeling others pain was easy for me.

High school years

As the years continued, my tics got worse. Not only was I shaking my head, blinking my eyes, sticking out my tongue, clearing my throat...I began making snorting sounds just like a pig! This was the worst of all the symptoms.

Home life kept getting worse. Shortly, before my sixteenth birthday, my mother finally had enough and kicked my father out of the house.

The abuse had to stop. She couldn't take anymore or someone was going to get seriously hurt or killed (probably her). Just before she packed his bags and threw them outside the front door, we had close family friends over for dinner. It must have been a special occasion because we never had visitors.

My parents began to argue (my father instigated it) and the next thing we heard was my mother screaming, "Run, get out of the house." My father threw a cast iron skillet at her head. "Call the police," she screamed. The police came and suggested my father leave and cool off.

A sick feeling deep in the pit of my stomach lasted for years after that evening. On the one hand, I hated my father and on the other, I still loved him and felt very sorry for him.

Unfortunately, my brother was the most affected! He started staying out all hours of the night and his grades got worse. He stuffed his bed to look like he was sleeping and snuck out of the house. Barna started drinking alcohol.

After throwing my father out, my mother filed for divorce. When the divorce was final, my father moved to California and remarried, a Hungarian woman named Marie. They eventually had my little sister, Judith.

My high school sweetheart

My mother, Barna and I were free. I started having friends over to the house for the first time since I started high school. My mother was meeting new friends and having fun.

During sophomore year, I met John. We became high school sweethearts and he took me to both the junior and senior prom. I couldn't believe one of the best looking guys in school with his own sports car wanted me as his girlfriend! John never asked what was wrong with me.

John and I were inseparable. It was only when I was with him that I felt safe, secure and free to be me. I was happy, in love and the symptoms seemed to lessen during high school. Maybe I just got better at controlling them.

In public, I was always on guard and aware of who was and wasn't watching. I grew eyes in the back of my head and my peripheral vision and hearing became acute. Most of my life I overheard people talking about me. Either to make fun of me or to try figuring out what was wrong with me. It was a full time job to try to control my symptoms (tics).

When the coast was clear and no one was watching, I let loose. All of the pent up twitches, jerks and noises came out. It felt so good, and so bad at the same time.

It felt like I was stuck in the same repetitive movements (almost like a seizure). Many times, I pulled my neck out of place by swiftly and forcefully jerking my neck to the side. The pain kept me from being able to turn my head for days.

Still, Tourette syndrome was not going to keep me down. I tried out for the cheerleading team but didn't make it because I tore the cartilage in my knee during final tryouts. I was devastated. After it healed, I tried out for the tennis team and made the junior varsity team. I played all through high school. Varsity was my goal, but I didn't make it.

It didn't bother me so much. It was a wonder I played tennis as well as I did. It took immense concentration and effort to keep my eyes on the ball. Imagine trying to swing a tennis racquet at a small tennis ball, while at the same time blinking and shaking your head...not easy!

I had a great time in high school while my brother sank deeper into himself and into trouble. My mother, bless her heart, worked so hard to provide for us that she would come home emotionally and physically drained. She could do little to discipline him.

My father never paid child support. For that matter, he never provided for our family. My high school graduation was bitter sweet. It was an important day in my life and my father promised he would be there. He never came.

College, here I come

My mother was always very supportive. She inspired both my brother and I to go to college. She knew an education would help us get further in life. When she was attending school in Hungary before her escape, she was Valedictorian of her class. My mother is very intelligent. When she came to the United States, all of her credits and credentials were disregarded. Speaking very little English and had no choice but to become a massage therapist. She loathed it, but it kept food on the table and a roof over our heads.

"Agi," she used to tell me, "You can do anything you set your mind to." Her words inspired me to believe I could do anything. After high school, Barna joined the armed forces and I went to community college.

It was during that time in my life, I began obsessing over my weight and taking diet pills. Not realizing it at the time, the ingredients in the pills heightened the symptoms of Tourette syndrome. I became jittery and couldn't focus on anything. I couldn't concentrate for more than a few minutes at a time. My thoughts skipped from one thing to another. I would sit down to do something and get right back up to do something else.

My moods also changed. I became irritable, nervous and angry. It became increasingly difficult for me to go to school. I began making louder noises and I couldn't control clearing my throat any longer. It became so embarrassing during exams because my classmates turned around and said, "Shush or stop it."

I dropped out of school numerous times. Each time my mother encouraged me to go back, so I did. I don't know how I did it. Two years turned into three and I was on my way to Arizona State University (ASU).

John, my high school sweetheart, was no longer my boyfriend. I had a few different boyfriends during college. It still surprises me that I even had boyfriends. They seemed to see past Tourette's. None of them asked me any questions as to why I was twitching, blinking, jerking my neck or clearing my throat.

During my first semester at Arizona State University, another embarrassing symptom of Tourette's manifested. I began to bark!

One afternoon, as I sat in the ASU library doing research for a class, a woman with tremendous courage approached me and said, "You have Tourette syndrome."

"No I don't," I replied, denying it (while on the inside I wanted to crawl into a hole and hide). Extremely puzzled, and probably embarrassed for approaching me, she walked away. I couldn't get out of the library fast enough, hoping she wouldn't see me.

Somehow, I managed to keep from barking in class. Although, the minute I was alone the barks let loose. I am so grateful my barks were like the barks of a cute little dog, not a big vicious one.

My major at ASU was Psychology and my goal was to help people solve their problems. Classes at ASU were larger than the community college, but now I sat in the back of the classes, instead of the front. I was more self conscious in college.

Almost made it!

The end was in sight with only a few credits to go. However, a few hurdles stood in my way. Math was always a struggle for me. The word problems got jumbled up in my mind, plus I just couldn't keep quiet during the examinations. I seemed to keep the sounds at bay in my other classes, but not during math class.

Determined to pass, I took the class three times, even getting a tutor the last time. I just couldn't do it. Why couldn't I tell the instructor I had Tourette syndrome? Why was I still so ashamed? Why didn't I ask if I could take the tests alone? The instructor probably would have let me. Unfortunately, I never graduated college.

My twenties

With no clear vision of the future, I felt lost. My twenties seemed surreal. I got mixed up with the wrong crowd and began to experiment with drugs. It was my excuse to escape reality and my life. It didn't work and symptoms of Tourette's got worse!

One of the happiest times during my mid-twenties was living in a Scottsdale condominium community. A mix of people lived there, mostly young professionals. I lived with a good friend and became our community's social coordinator.

At the time, I worked at a local grocery store as a cashier. You would think with my obvious physical symptoms of Tourette's that I would not want to be so visible. The job paid very well and I wasn't going to let

Tourette's keep me from making a good living. I got really good at controlling the head shaking, twitching, blinking and barking. Luckily for me, by that time, the urge to bark was very mild and I could contain it until I was alone. One of my fondest memories and a boost to my self-esteem came during this time. The grocery store chain held a contest to identify the fastest cashier in Phoenix. The prize for first place was $50.00 and I won!

Working part time at this grocery store allowed me to live in this popular community. It was wonderful. No one made fun of me and everyone accepted me. I was beginning to accept myself. Life was pretty good.

During one of our famous parties my brother stumbled in uninvited and incoherently drunk. I couldn't believe it. Just when I was beginning to be happy and forget my problems, there he was to remind me all over again. For the next twelve years, Barna would be either homeless wandering the streets near where I lived or in jail. It hurt so badly that I could hardly stand it. Every time I heard a siren I thought, "Is he dead or going to jail?"

No one knew how miserable I was. Just like Cinderella, ever since I was a little girl, I dreamed of "Prince Charming" coming and rescuing me. From as early on as I can remember, I have repeated over and over in my mind the words, "I deserve to be happy." Somehow, I always knew that one day my dreams would come true.

What a hypocrite, I was

A six-foot tall, athletically built, soccer player and young professional was coming to pick me up for our first date. We went to dinner and a movie and got along famously. He was funny, kind, considerate, a gentleman (opened my car door) and filled with ambition. There was only one thing wrong.

Can you guess what that was? Right...he also had Tourette syndrome! He seemed to be in the same place of denial that I was and didn't initiate conversation about Tourette. I even noticed when he thought I wasn't looking, that he made the same jerking movements I did.

It's so funny looking back at it now. When he wasn't looking, I would get my few seconds of releasing pent up twitches and jerks. Most likely, he also had exceptional peripheral vision and knew I was doing the same bizarre things he was. Neither one of us was going to admit it.

Surprisingly, he called me for a second date (I was sure he wouldn't). I told him he was a really nice guy and made up some excuse why I couldn't see him again. What a shame...I didn't even give him a chance. What a hypocrite! I was embarrassed for myself and too embarrassed to have a boyfriend with Tourette syndrome.

My thirties

Months before my thirtieth birthday, my brother and I reunited with my father. When my father didn't come to my high school graduation, I was angry. I called him and said, "I hate you. You are not my father." All that changed in a heartbeat, the minute I set foot off the plane. There he was, nervously anticipating my arrival.

With tears in my eyes, I hugged him like we had been a loving father and daughter our entire lives. He was still my dad and I loved him very much. All was forgiven. Unfortunately, his health was failing. He had lost the sight of one eye, had excruciating back pain, and his liver was failing. Alcohol was killing him. My brother and I spent a week with him, my little sister, Judith, and her mother, Marie.

Many times during the week I saw my father and brother embracing. I knew my father was giving him the love he so desperately needed. Barna was so happy watching over our father just like a mother hen. He bought him an assortment of vitamins hoping to help him regain his health.

After a few days, I began to sense something was wrong. My father gave Barna and I all of his jewelry and hundreds of dollars. "Why", I asked. "I've never given you and Barna anything. Now I want to," he answered. He handed me a heart shaped pendant on a delicate gold chain and said, "I bought this for Judy, for her birthday but I won't be giving it to her." He seemed so sad.

As my brother and I were beginning to say our goodbyes, Judy whispered in my ear, "Agi, I'm afraid, take me with you." Kneeling down, holding her hands and looking into her desperate eyes I asked, "What are you afraid of?" She replied, "I'm afraid Apu is going to do something bad." Reassuringly I said, "No he won't. All of our lives he threatened to do bad things to us, but he never did."

Understanding her feelings of fear and insecurity, all I wanted to do was pick her up into my arms and take her back to Arizona with me. Judy was so nervous at home. Her fear and insecurities manifested themselves by her pulling out her eyelashes. She reminded me of me, when I was her age. I should have seen the warning signs!!!

Judy was a child actress. She appeared in an after school special entitled, "Losing A Sister" produced by Henry Winkler and acted along side of Michael Caine in "Jaws 4". She loved being a movie star and I loved that she was one. I should have brought her home with me.

One week later, my mother, brother and I got the shocking news. They were all dead. My father shot Marie in the hallway of their home and shot Judy while she was still in her bed. He then poured gasoline over their bodies and burnt them. Afterwards, he committed suicide by shooting himself in the head.

I found out later that child protective services were going to remove Judy from the home. The neighbors reported they heard my father threatening to kill Marie several times in the front yard. Upon reflection, I am certain my father thought, "If I can't keep my little girl, no one can."

My mother, brother and I were devastated. Just when there was hope my brother would stop drinking, my father did the unimaginable. As for me, the world seemed to make no sense. I felt sick and completely lost, again.

Turning point in my life

My mother continued to give me information about Tourette syndrome. Still, I didn't want to acknowledge it. My thirtieth birthday was just around the corner. Little did I know, the turning point in my life was about to present itself.

It began on my thirtieth birthday on the beach in San Diego with my new boyfriend, Dale. I closed my eyes to make my usual wish for happiness and freedom. Taking a huge breath in, I blew out all of the candles on my one-of-a -kind sand castle cake.

Dale was a Godsend. Not only did he free me from a life with no direction, he freed me from the shame of Tourette syndrome. Yes, can you believe it? Finally I was to come out with all of it! One day he casually said, "Agi, I want to understand why you do what you do." As you can imagine by my past denials, I was squirming to get out of the discussion. I couldn't get out of this one. Tears welled up in my eyes and I answered his questions.

For the first time in my life, I told someone everything. How it felt, how it hurt, how embarrassed I was. How I ended relationships abruptly, so as to never get into the discussion we were having at that moment.

He held my hand and listened compassionately. Unbelievably, I even told him about the obsessive-compulsive rituals I experienced at that time. For example, before opening the car door, I had to...and I mean had to...touch the handle of the car door just right before I could open it. It usually took 20-30 attempts.

It was like being stuck in the motion. It had to feel just right before I could open the car door. I also began to stammer, almost stutter, during my late twenties and into my early thirties. This was possibly the most annoying of all of the symptoms I had experienced up until then. The words got stuck at the base of my throat and struggled to come out.

After an emotional two hours spent confessing all of my pent up feelings of shame, I felt like a three hundred pound weight was lifted off of my shoulders. My whole life opened up after that day. My confidence and self-esteem increased 100% and peace...indescribable peace came over me. Dale commented that my face looked different. I wasn't on guard anymore. From then on, anyone who asked what was wrong with me got an honest answer.

A few months after that freeing experience, the entrepreneur side of me surfaced. My mother always said I could do anything I set my mind to. That year, I met a physician who had a dream of offering mobile mammography to women in the workplace. He believed in my abilities to promote his vision. We created Mobile On Site Mammography (M.O.M.) and it continues to be offered in Arizona today.

After five and a half years together, my relationship ended with Dale. He was a gift to me for exactly that time in my life. I was ready to take on the future...twitching and single! It was time to find myself and discover my purpose in the world...without a man...for the time being.

Ready to conquer the world

Leasing agent and concierge was my title at the San Marin Luxury Apartments in Scottsdale. It was the best job I'd ever had. The apartments were home to young professionals, as well as, business people relocating to Arizona. I was meeting new people everyday and organizing social gatherings for the residents. Tourette syndrome didn't bother me anymore and it didn't seem to bother anyone else. Truly, I was free.

Then one day, to my surprise, the happiest man I had ever seen walked through the front doors of our leasing office. I took him on a tour of the property and showed him a few open apartments. Within weeks, we were dating.

During one of our intimate discussions, Bill said the most refreshing words, "Agi, I will never try to change anything about you." Wow! I was dating the most unconditional man I had ever met.

Was I dating the "Prince Charming" I had been waiting for my entire life? Bill was thirteen years older than me and there was undeniable magnetism between us. We talked and kissed for hours on the balcony of his apartment. His lips were made for mine! This was the beginning of a wonderful life together.

Bill was away on business when one of my co-workers knocked on the door. I opened the door and knew instantly something was wrong. "Call your mother right away," she said. I knew it was about Barna. My mother answered the phone. "Barna is dead. Come over," she cried.

His lifeless body was discovered in a Scottsdale canal. The coroner said he was drunk at the time he drowned. What a tragedy. All it would have taken for my brother to live his life was to have his father back again. It was such a waste of an intelligent and sensitive person. My mother did her best to substitute in place of my father. <u>There is no substitution.</u>

A boy needs his father or a positive male role model. Fathers must realize the importance of their involvement in the lives of their sons!

> ➢ If your child does not have a positive role model, find one. There are many resources available including the Big Brother programs and mentoring programs. Do not wait until it is too late. You can make a difference!

> ➢ The 'power of your words', are very important to a child's personal growth and self- esteem. It's not only limited to kids with ADD, ADHD or Tourette syndrome. My father never verbally abused me, but he did Barna. My brother fulfilled my father's prophecy that he would never amount to anything and he was a failure. Discover how you can change your words to become positive building blocks for yourself, as well as, for children beginning on page 113.

Both my father and my brother were dead. Finally, I felt freed from anxiety and fear. The worry and deep sadness I carried my entire life was finally gone. I was thirty-six years old and ready to have a healthy relationship with a man who was everything I was looking for. Above all, a man who accepted me completely for who I was and who I was not.

It was during this time when another symptom of Tourette's manifested itself. Under my breath the words F---k, F---k, F---k came out. Always in three's...go figure.

As the years went by, other words joined this sequence. Boy, did this get me in trouble. Many times I would try to control myself from saying these curse words but..oops..they came out during the most inappropriate times. Most often times, just after the voice on the other end of the phone answered, "Hello."

The person would hang up. I'd call them back and apologize and tell them about Tourette's. I giggle when I think about it now. Still today, I can't quite shake this one.

I've thought over and over again why I blurt out curse words. I've concluded that even though I have accepted Tourette's and am no longer ashamed or embarrassed by it, the symptoms are still very frustrating.

Curse words are angry words. Maybe it's my frustration and anger at Tourette syndrome. The anger manifests itself through cursing. Fortunately, the curse words come out very gently and softly. I don't holler them at the top of my lungs.

A blessing in disguise

A few months after Barna died, I began experiencing what I thought were anxiety attacks. The palms of my hands began to sweat, my heart throbbed and I felt close to passing out. One night, it scared me enough to get me to see the doctor. A urine test revealed sugar in my urine. The doctor looked alarmed and told me I needed further testing for possible diabetes. Well, I never did go back for the tests. It was too soon after Barna's death and I just didn't want to deal with one more bit of bad news.

My mother couldn't take any more bad news. All I wanted to do was continue to indulge in my comfort foods, which included: Cake, chocolate, cheese, bread, soda, champagne and hamburgers...lot's of all of the above.

My diet was awful. The only salad I ate was iceberg lettuce with sliced steak on top. I woke up to a can of soda and went to bed with a piece of cake or some sort of dessert. I drank only one glass of water each day (sometimes not even that much). I continued this way for the next few years.

Gradually, I noticed my left breast was looking different. The nipple was not getting erect and there was puckering to the side of it. I underwent a needle biopsy, after a mammogram and ultra sound showed no abnormality.

On July 11, 1997, my wake-up call came. The radiologist who performed the needle biopsy two days before called and said, "Agi, I'm sorry. I have bad news. Your biopsy shows a carcinoma, breast cancer."

Wouldn't you know, it was a type of cancer that was not easily treatable with traditional treatment. The prognosis was poor, even with chemotherapy and surgery. I chose a different path to heal myself. If you would like to read the complete story about my healing journey and exactly how I got well following a natural healing program, read my book entitled, "Triumph Over Cancer, A Natural Approach."

Cancer turned out to be a blessing in my life. It shocked me into living my life differently. First, I gained a real sense for my life and how quickly it can be taken away. I became grateful for being alive another day. With this gratitude came an inner strength I never knew existed. There was so much to live for and so much more fun to have. It was not my time to go.

A change in diet

A healthy diet was key to healing from cancer. To my surprise, with a change in diet came a dramatic change in Tourette's. Symptoms almost disappeared!

For the first six weeks of the natural healing program, I juiced organic carrots, parsley, apples, celery and ginger along with other combinations of vegetables including spinach, broccoli and beets. I drank several cleansing and detoxifications teas, nutrition drinks and herbal formulas. After six weeks, I added raw and cooked vegetables, fruits, whole grains, nuts and seeds to my diet.

No meat, dairy, white flour, processed sugar or processed foods touched my lips for the first year of my natural healing program. My diet was very boring because I didn't know how to cook at the time, but that has changed. Today, I create exciting and delicious recipes using fresh ingredients.

Before cancer, I felt I couldn't function in the morning without an iced cappuccino, soda, or get through the day without a piece of chocolate. I believe that as a result of a diet high in mucous forming foods I suffered with severe allergies and sinus infections. From my early twenties until the diagnosis, I survived the ongoing battle by habitually taking over-the-counter allergy medications and steroid injections.

Every time I took an allergy medication, including antihistamines, Tourette symptoms got worse! I became irritable and moody. The head jerking got so bad, to the point where if I jerked too hard, I would hear a crunch and get dizzy. So many times I thought I would break my neck, if I jerked just a little bit harder.

I was also aware that symptoms worsened when I drank coffee and ate foods with sugar, but I was addicted and couldn't give them up. What I didn't know at the time, until I studied to become an herbalist, was that caffeine and food additives like M.S.G. and excitotoxins were aggravating my symptoms even more.

It's been over five years since I've changed my diet and I've never felt better. Symptoms of Tourette's have lessened tremendously. People who have known me for years comment on how much better I am.

My attention span increased by leaps and bounds. I can actually sit down and complete a task without having to get up every few minutes to do something else. My focus is clear. The easiest way to explain my clear focus is that it feels like a film has been removed from my eyes and I can see clearer than ever before.

One of the most frightening symptoms I used to experience was the feeling of disconnectedness. The only time this feeling reappears now is after eating or drinking something that had MSG, excitotoxins or sulfites in it. It feels like I have been drugged. A headache or sudden fatigue accompanies the feeling of disconnectedness.

I don't often eat out because it's hard to know what additives are being used to prepare the foods. Fortunately, my husband and I have discovered restaurants that use only fresh ingredients and have become loyal patrons.

In the past, before even looking at the appetizers and main courses listed on the menu, I would go directly to the dessert section. Any dessert with chocolate in it sparked my attention. Many times, my dining experience started with dessert! Today is a much different story. Chocolate doesn't interest me in the least. As a matter of fact, now when I eat chocolate, I get a headache. The severity depends on how much chocolate or what type

I've eaten. The choice is easy. Do I want to feel good or do I want to suffer with a headache? I choose to feel good.

In the past, I never gave wheat allergies much thought. Yet today, because I am aware of how food affects Tourette's and my mood, I've noticed wheat also triggers symptoms. Many times after eating something with wheat I feel irritable, congested and my attention span is very limited. Although, when I eat something made with <u>sprouted wheat</u> these symptoms don't appear.

I believe it would be very beneficial for anyone who shows symptoms of ADD, ADHD or Tourette syndrome (or for that matter mood swings and headaches) to get tested for food allergies. Food allergies can cause a wide range of symptoms that may be mistaken for symptoms of attention deficit and disruptive disorders.

Look at me now!

On September 4, 2002, I will be forty-four years old. For the first time in my life, I am comfortable in my own shoes. No longer ashamed or self-conscious about having Tourette syndrome. I am happily married to a man who accepts me with or without Tourette syndrome.

Food does not control my life any longer (that in itself is a miracle). I make healthier choices on a daily basis and have been rewarded with a physical sense of well-being and an inner sense of peace. As I mentioned, symptoms of Tourette syndrome and ADD have lessened dramatically. I can sit still, concentrate and focus.

My self-confidence and self-esteem are firmly, yet humbly grounded. I have accomplished writing this my second book and I am traveling across the country to deliver the message of hope. Tourette syndrome has been a blessing, not the curse I always thought it was.

Every morning before getting out of bed I thank God for my life. Then without hesitation, I pray the "Prayer of Jabez".

The Jabez Prayer

And Jabez called on the God of Israel saying,

"Oh, that You would bless me indeed,
and enlarge my territory,
that Your hand would be with me,
and that You would keep me from evil,
that I may not cause pain!"

So God granted him what he requested.

1 Chronicles 4:10 (NKJV)

chapter 2

Proactive Mom

"Listen to advice, accept correction,
to be the wiser in the time to come"

Lene took initiative and learned everything she could about diet and how it affected her son's mood and behavior. Through unconditional love, perseverance and communication, Lene was able to help her son without the use of prescription drugs.

"Children are wonderful! We can learn so much from them. My experience with my oldest son, through his early years, has taught me more about food and diet than I ever thought possible. Being my first born, it was hard to know which behaviors were normal and which were not. As his social life became busier, I noticed there were differences between his behavior and other children.

I would describe him from the ages of 1 - 4 as a very busy, happy and social child. He was talking in three word sentences by the age of one. During the ages of 3 - 6, I would describe him as somewhat restless, irritable and cranky. He threw temper tantrums out of frustration. He was strong willed. He would not sit still for very long, compared to other children his age. His focus shifted often onto multiple activities.

At the age of 6, we had him tested for hyperactivity and ADD. This was after 6 months of kindergarten experience. My husband and I were told by social professionals our son had symptoms of hyperactivity, but could very well grow out of it. We agreed NOT to place him on medications at this point in time.

I didn't want my child to be labeled as having a "problem" or to take medication/chemicals, to treat symptoms, when I believed that there must be other solutions to remedy his condition.

An extraordinary teacher creates solutions - the "Working Bureau" and the "Listening Chair"

During that year, we had great communication with his teacher. A wonderful woman, who came up with some creative ideas to help our child focus on class activities throughout the day.

She invented a "Working Bureau" just for him. It was a 3-wall cardboard separator, his separate office in the class. It helped him stay on task with assigned paper work without getting distracted.

The teacher also gave him his own special "listening chair" during circle time. This was the time when the class would get together in a circle to learn. As the teacher put it, "This will allow the other children to have a chance to participate as well."

My son was the constant voice answering every question. He was a fast learner and eager to share information. My son's hand was in the air, answering questions from the teacher more than necessary. The "listening chair" worked really well for him, because he felt special and he absolutely loved the attention. It also got him conditioned to listening more, rather than answering all the time.

It became a privilege for other children in the class to be allowed to sit next to him. This teacher really knew how to motivate and make the kids feel at their best. Most of my son's teachers described him as a very enthusiastic and social child, but lacking in self-control.

During the next 2 years, we had his teachers make "sticker charts" on his desk, so he would be reminded to stay on task. The stickers (pictures of happy faces or sunshine or sports) worked to motivate him most of the time. He always knew how many stickers he had earned and where his progress was in focusing and listening.

By the 3rd grade, he was not so lucky with his teacher. It had a really negative effect on him. There was little stimulation in the classroom and his teacher just didn't know how to communicate with children or their parents.

As parents, we tried several times to communicate with this teacher and the principal, but not much changed. He went from being on top of the world to having very little self-confidence.

He became very hard on himself. He didn't feel that he fit in and wrote self-destructive notes on how he "hated himself and wished he were never born." He started to hate school and broke down in tears at home. He became angry and frustrated. It just broke our hearts.

My son just couldn't understand why he felt this way. We were advised to have him tested for the gifted program and he passed with very high marks in more than one subject. I also contacted the school child psychologist.

Our "happy boy" was coming back

He saw the school child psychologist every week. Over time, we saw little sparks of our "happy boy" coming back. It took the school year to work it through, but it taught my son how important it is to express what you feel. My son learned the importance of communicating how he felt to others. He began to gain a sense of self worth. He was always very sensitive and was given great advice on how to deal with that as well.

That year we got him involved in many sports. He played three different sports. People told us we were nuts to have him so busy with sports. Our son needed to stay active. It was a good outlet for his energy and he excelled in every sport. I believe it is a good idea to keep children who are hyperactive busy with activities. Sports also helped bring his confidence back.

I started researching diets and how they affect behavior. The first book I came across was entitled, "The ADD & ADHD Diet", written by Rachel Bell and Dr. Howard Pieper. From reading it, I learned that many scientists and nutritionists believe food allergies cause many of our health and behavioral challenges.

The first step I took, in helping my son through diet, was to begin lowering his sugar intake. That included fruits and fruit juices. He ate bananas and apples in moderation. I diluted fruit juices by adding 50% water. Soda was not available in our home. However, during certain occasions (birthday parties, etc.) my son would be allowed to have a little, as long as it was diluted with water.

I also cut back on starches such as snacks (chips, cheese flavored crackers, pretzels, and cookies) and replaced them with protein bars, baby carrot sticks, some cheese and red grapes. He mostly drank water. Among his favorite foods were apples, bananas, mini turkey sandwiches, canned mackerel in tomato sauce and pate sandwiches.

After experiencing some positive changes in his behavior, we decided to cut back on more foods. The next to go was milk and most cereals. We replaced milk with rice milk and sometimes with soymilk. I got both of my kids liking these milks over a 6-week period by diluting our regular milk with these new milks, until one day they didn't know the difference.

By the time my son was 8, I discovered a supplement called "attention focus for kids." They were gel caps containing vitamin E, fish oils and evening primrose oil. We kept seeing improvement including a reduction in his mood swings, and less headaches. His behavior even got better at school. He became more focused on his tasks. My son also began to take supplements of Zinc Citrate (three days a week), B6 and Vitamin C.

Some days were more challenging than others. Slowly and surely, we could look at what he ate and how his behavior changed. It was truly amazing for my husband and I to witness the differences in his behavior and mood by what foods he ate.

My son was very fond of "chicken nuggets" (fried chicken from fast food establishments). I was set on finding foods that I could make for him that would look and taste similar to the "nuggets". Reading about fish oils and how they are essential for brain and eye function led me to creating "salmon nuggets", a huge hit and something I made 2 to 3 times per week. I believe that children need to eat more fish. A way to make it more to their liking would be to make a hollandaise sauce, some melted butter or Ranch Dressing with it.

He was not fond of vegetables and I wanted to increase his vegetable intake. So, I experimented with a few ingredients and created "vegetable and meatball marinara". The meats I used were ground buffalo, turkey, lamb and sometimes pork. All of these meats when mixed with the vegetables have the consistency that reminds children of the typical "meatball".

Another well-liked recipe in my family is "French vegetable soup", which became part of our regular dinner menu. This simple fresh and tasty soup along with garlic croutons and fresh Parmesan cheese (not in the can) was a nutritious meal. I knew how important garlic was for good health so I cooked with lots of fresh garlic (two to three bulbs a week).

As we learned about the different foods and how we reacted to them, we explained it to our children so they could make better choices when we would not be around. This was important for them to know at their friend's birthday parties, play dates and school because often the snacks were filled with sugar and starches.

With these changes we could clearly see the difference. Our child calmed down and became more cooperative. He did better in school and did not feel different than the other children anymore.

He was no longer misunderstood by his teachers or by his peers. Luckily, for him, he was and is academically very strong, so as long as he was challenged, there would be more cooperation in the classroom.

Communication is important

Thankfully, there are wonderful teachers out there with great ideas to help children who do not necessarily fit the "norm". As a mother, all I wanted to do was to help this talented child grow up to be confident and to succeed at the challenges life would give him.

For a child, being different and labeled can be a very painful experience. I think that negative attention is often given to children with these symptoms, which is the last thing they need.

We are NOT all the same. We interpret, feel and react to things differently. Maybe what we can learn to do is try to understand and show more tolerance and compassion for each other. We need to stop labeling and isolating children and people that do not fit into a typically accepted category.

The key for parents to succeed in helping their children is to keep in constant communication with their teachers and keep communication open at home. Today, my son is 11 and starting 7th grade. He has really come a long way and we are so proud of him.

He has calmed down so much and stays focused on his work at school and at home."

• Lene's recipes appear in the Lidle Café cookbook.

chapter 3

Bridging The Communication Gap

"The way
to greater light
leads through darkness"

"At first, I thought my son, Lance, was just a very
annoying little fellow. Very sweet, very affectionate but
very annoying. I remember hearing myself say, "You
have to stop these annoying habits before they get harder
and harder to break." I must have said it multiple times a
day. Lance would just give me a blank stare. He wasn't
even aware he was doing anything different from other
children!

We might be at the movies and he would be doing
this...cough, sniff, cough, sniff, cough, sniff...until neither
we nor those around us could hear the movie. When I'd
tell him to be quiet...blank stare. "What was I doing,
Mommy?"

I had never heard of Tourette syndrome until one
evening when the children were in bed and my husband
and I were watching our favorite TV show "Quincy."
(My goodness, I learned a lot from that show). That
particular episode was about a woman with Tourette's.

As I watched, my eyes were opened to the fact that
this was probably what my son had. The next day I went
to the library. For hours I looked for information on this

condition, but all I found was a tiny paragraph in the dictionary.

Lance was in second grade at this time. His teacher was concerned that his eyesight was poor because he was constantly squinting his eyes very tightly. She sent him to the nurse's office to have his eyes tested. She recognized immediately the symptoms he exhibited were the same symptoms associated with Tourette syndrome.

He brought home a note and two articles dealing with Tourette's. The note said simply, "I think your son has this." His pediatrician had no idea what "this" was and sent us to a pediatric neurologist.

This was very interesting, as most of the office visit the doctor sat in the waiting room watching Lance as he played with toys and other children. He confirmed what the nurse and I thought. He suggested we don't do anything until it becomes a problem in Lance's life.

Name-calling can be so cruel

Problems arose about six months later. Lance was suspended from school for fighting. He was tired of the other kids calling him "Turtle Boy" on the playground, because of his habit of pulling his neck in and out, then stretching it out. The doctor prescribed Haldol. He told us to tell the teacher Lance would not be able to do his work as well, because his movements would be much slowed by this medication.

The teachers in elementary school worked with him. They gave him special assignments, such as doing every other problem instead of every one. Only once did he have a problem with a teacher, who was very angry with him for making noises in class. She had not read his student record and felt terrible when it was brought to her attention.

Junior high was a different story. Not all of his teachers were willing to give him the extra attention he needed. In fact, at the end of the 7th grade, we received a note telling us that Lance would have to do 7th grade over again. I knew this was ridiculous. I knew how smart he was. I took him to be tested and he tested at the college level in all subjects. The school admitted there must have been a mistake and let him go on to the 8th grade.

I learned a very valuable lesson

It was necessary for me to be at the school and aware of his classes and assignments. He was not able to concentrate or remember well because of the medication. I got a job working in the library.

The next year, high school, I typed a form letter telling the teachers all about Tourette syndrome and Haldol. I made sure they knew exactly what this condition was and what problems occurred because of it and the medication.

I made copies and put one in each teacher's box. In each classroom, a helper was seated next to Lance to make sure he had the assignment and most of the time to help try to keep him awake (side effect of medication). I learned a valuable lesson by being in communication with his teachers. Without the communication, Lance may have been even more misunderstood.

He missed 1st period so many times; he had to be home schooled for a few subjects in order to graduate. I worked at the phone company by now and arranged my schedule around getting Lance to school in the morning. All of these problems were not the result of Tourette syndrome, but the result of the medication.

His medication was switched to Chlonodine in the 10th grade. He wore a patch. So the 1st day, he would sleep all day, but no symptoms. By the fifth day, his symptoms were raging. It was a struggle to figure out which was worse, the Tourette syndrome or the medications. I always let Lance decide if he wanted the medication or not. Many times he would choose not to take it and end up in fights. He was suspended many times for fighting (kids can be so cruel).

About five years ago, I began to learn about herbs and alternative approaches to healing. My turning to herbs was a result of my older son's, Kevin's, migraine headaches. My son's migraine headaches are completely gone with the use of acupressure. I had no idea, earlier in life, how diet could affect both of my son's symptoms. I wish I did.

This was about the same time Lance decided to stop taking any meds at all. He decided to "live with" the symptoms and had a job where everyone loved him and didn't make fun of him. He was "safe".

At 19, he left for Portugal to serve a mission for our church. A few months into his mission, I received a heart-wrenching letter from him. He wanted to try herbs. He had started making a "barking" noise and people on the street were actually crossing over to the other side of the street to avoid him! He wasn't upset for himself, but he didn't want to make others uncomfortable.

I sent Lance an herbal formula called Attention Calm. He said it helped him a lot. It was soon after this that he wrote me to tell me about his change of feelings concerning his Tourette's. He said he had embraced it. He knew it had been given to him to help him learn and grow. It was an important part of him. He had more compassion for others, because of it. He was actually thankful for it.

Lance was married in January to a wonderful girl who thinks the sun rises and sets on him. He doesn't worry about his symptoms, but lives with them.

chapter 4

Mother On A Mission

"When the student
is ready
the teacher will appear"

*"If you can't control them, drug them" is an all too familiar
pattern of treatment a growing number of people are beginning to
question. Stephanie, a thirty-six year old single mother from
Texas, is one of these people. In this chapter, you will hear the
testimony of an empowered mother on a mission to help her
child.*

"I really think my nine year old son, Stephen, was
always hyperactive. I just didn't want to admit that he
could have anything wrong with him. No parent wants
anything to be wrong with his or her child. Looking back,
I noticed a difference in his behavior when he was three.
It was very hard to capture his attention. I just thought he
was still a baby and very busy exploring.

The most agitating behavior was when he acted like
he couldn't hear me! I asked him to do something and it
would literally take 10–15 minutes to capture his
attention. Stephen got wound up and started running
around. It would take forever to calm him down.

He was constantly moving or messing with
something. The mood swings were terrible. It didn't take

anything to make him mad. He would throw things, stomp off, scream, yell, and slam doors.

It was like he would deliberately do things he knew he wasn't supposed to do. He knew it was wrong, because he would always say he was "sorry" and didn't know why he had done them. He meant it from the bottom of his heart.

When Stephen was in kindergarten, his teacher would tell me what disruptive things he was doing. I just apologized and said I would talk to him, hoping and praying that he would stop. It wasn't until the first grade that the bomb was dropped in my life.

His teacher had a child that was ADHD and noticed Stephen had the same symptoms. She helped me with different testing methods and counseling before I ever went to a doctor. I took him to the doctor at the end of the first grade. He diagnosed Stephen with ADHD.

I blamed myself over and over for Stephen's condition. What did I do wrong? I felt like I was being punished for something I had done wrong and was paying for it through my child. With God's help, I got through it. God would never use a child like that to punish a person.

He's my child, I have to help him

So, I began to put all of my energy into helping Stephen. I began by asking his first grade teacher if she knew of a teacher in the second grade that understood how to cope with an ADHD child. Thank God his second grade teacher also had a child who was ADHD. She was excellent with him and always kept me informed of everything. She was forever letting me know it was going to be okay. I was a basket case and couldn't believe there was something wrong with my child.

His second grade teacher suggested a drug named Cylert. It was the drug that her son did well on, for a while. A while is the key phrase. We started on a low dosage, 9 or 10mg. After a couple of months, it just wasn't doing anything. The doctor raised the dosage over the months and Stephen began taking two Cylert's every day.

It still wasn't working. The side effects were worse. When the drug wore off by the evening, he was back to his mood swings, tamper tantrums, and loud outbursts. I told the doctor, he had to change the medicine.

The next drug he put him on was a nightmare. It was Ritalin, 10mgs. I had hoped and prayed so hard that Ritalin would be the one drug we could stay away from. I really didn't see a choice because he was so out of control. After a week it wasn't really doing much good, so the doctor upped the dose just to see. He thought he might not be getting enough of the drug to be doing anything. Now Stephen was on 20mgs, one dose before school and another dose at lunchtime.

I couldn't stand it. I had to take one of those pills to see exactly how it made him feel!

I am extremely hyper as well and sometimes think I might have been ADHD when I was younger. Then it dawned on me...what does the drug make Stephen feel like? I never thought to take any of Stephen's drugs before to see what effects I would feel.

So, I took a Ritalin and was appalled at how it affected me. I felt sluggish, depressed, out of it, and had no energy whatsoever.

If this was happening to me, and I'm quite a bit larger than Stephen, how must this drug be affecting him? Very concerned, I called the doctor and asked him if Stephen might be experiencing the same symptoms I was. He said, "Yes."

The doctor then prescribed Paxil for his depression. Okay, this is where we draw the line. I was not going to put him on that. He wasn't depressed. The Ritalin was too much and basically causing him to be non-functional.

I asked Stephen's teacher if she knew of any non-narcotic drugs to treat ADHD. She told me she had known of some children being on Concerta. It didn't have as many side effects, could last up to 14 hours, and it didn't always stay in the system until you took the next pill.

I began to do some research and felt like Concerta was a better alternative to all the other drugs he had tried. I told the doctor that I wanted Stephen on Concerta. He prescribed it.

The doctor didn't spend much time with Stephen. He pretty much went on what the teachers, counselors, and I were telling him. Each time Stephen was on a different drug he did better for a week or so. His biggest problem was being focused for long periods of time.

Keeping him from playing, talking and giggling in his classroom was the hardest thing to get him to stop doing. Schoolwork is hard for him because it takes too long and he can't sit still long enough to do it. At home, it's like pulling teeth to get him to do homework. NONE of the pills helped him stay focused for very long.

Stephen has been wonderful through this whole ordeal. He is the most loving and caring child I know, and not just because he's mine. Everyone says the same thing.

He knew something was wrong with him, faced it, and did anything I thought was right for him. That's why I have worked so hard trying to find something that was not going to harm my child. He is so smart, has a huge kind heart, and cares so much about doing well for himself and others.

Stephen is willing to try anything to be better. Who wouldn't care so much with that kind of effort from a child? What tears my heart apart is when he tells me "sorry" for the things he does. He hates it when he can't control himself from being angry and it makes him miserable.

A new beginning

Stephen, his older sister, Amaris, and I moved to Phoenix, Arizona in February 2002. My stepmother, Mary, eats mainly natural foods and began to share information with me. "I'll give it a try," I thought.

I first began to make healthier choices by giving Stephen more water and noticed a huge improvement. He knows how much it will help him and makes sure, on his own, to have as much water as he can hold in a day. He's less sluggish and tired feeling.

Stephen has learned to read the labels on foods. What ingredients to look for that he shouldn't have. He always looks for MSG (which is in almost everything), yellow, red and blue colorings, and other ingredients like wheat and sugar.

He gets disheartened when he finds something he likes, but then reads the label and finds one of the above ingredients. Then our mission begins to search for a substitute he can have.

When you read the labels you find out just how unnecessary all those ingredients really are. Our foods are filled with preservatives, additives and fillers. Who's to say how much of it is really FOOD? I used to think, "They would never put foods on the market that would hurt me, but they do." You may not take my word for it, and I don't want you to. Go ahead, find out for yourself.

I have read that if you really want to eat healthier, start eating the way they did in the 40's. Fresh foods, not canned, boxed or wrapped. We are becoming pickled and preserved, even before GOD has said it is time to go.

We've even discovered an herbal formula to help him focus and be calmer. Stephen is no longer on medication and prefers to be on an herbal formula.

He has become calmer, easier to communicate with and is trying to pay attention more to his behaviors. He says the former pills made him feel like he was getting too much medicine all at once.

In other words, they are too strong. The herbal formula just takes the edge off of things. This allows him to help himself learn how to control himself. He's also gaining more self-confidence by controlling his temper.

Sunday night through Friday after school, Stephen is on a fairly strict and healthy diet. He doesn't get soda, anything with sugar, food colorings and MSG's. Come Friday after school he can choose two different things he wants to eat. He gets two on Friday, two on Saturday and two on Sunday. Starting again Sunday at dinnertime, he is right back on his healthy diet.

This schedule really works because he looks forward to his choices for the weekend. What I'm seeing is that he doesn't crave the sugars and sweets as much.

Stephen told his teacher that he couldn't have any sugar or soda, Monday through Friday. He did this all by himself. I never thought he would take so quickly to getting off sugar and soda. Stephen tells me he wants to feel better, so he is willing to do what it takes. As parents, we need to communicate with our children on this level.

Children are our responsibility

I believe we brought these helpless souls into the world and it is our responsibility to do everything possible for them until they decide to leave home.

Stephen has ADHD and that's just something I have to put on my priority list. My responsibility is to see it through, no matter what the cost. I'm not going to be the reason my children don't make it in this world. They know I will always be there for them.

My example is important, so I've been eating the same healthy foods as Stephen and drinking more water along with him, I feel so much better. I'm losing weight, I'm not sluggish in the afternoons and my skin is so smooth. Water is playing a big part in both of our health improvements.

Just water alone improved Stephen's concentration and hyperactivity. He tells me his memory is even better. I feel encouraged and empowered by educating myself and educating Stephen. We are taking charge. Now the challenge comes when Stephen is at his dad's for the summer.

Stephen was eight months old when his father and I divorced. He has always been around his dad as much as possible and stays with him for the summer. Having a mother and a father is very important for a child.

I typed up information about ADHD to inform his father of Stephen's condition. I'm even sending a box full of snacks for him to eat. The herbal formula is being packed too. It's a step in the right direction for us both. I know God is holding my hand through this and I won't stop looking for more answers.

Changing your paradigm

Years ago, I attended a seminar on management skills. The speaker was talking about change. Beginning with how to do things differently and how to try new ideas for improving employee's attitudes.

The message focused on "Changing Your Paradigm." He shared that most people never think they have the option to change the way they do things, so they become stuck in the same rut day after day. Doing the same things they have been doing for most of their lives.

That day, the seed was planted in my head. First, I had to start with me! I had to change my paradigm, the way I was used to thinking, to achieve the positive results I was hoping to see with Stephen. I had to be happy with myself, so my children could have a positive example. If I was going to expect Stephen to give up certain foods then I had to give them up too. We've been out of our rut and into this new healthy lifestyle for only three months. The results are very positive.

Today, I don't worry as much and I move beyond the negative. I look for the positive in all situations. My mind is no longer clogged with despair and depression.

During this process, I discovered that the things I had success in changing, fit with who I was and wanted to be. It never worked before when I tried changing myself to be what someone else wanted me to be.

This move to Arizona was my opportunity to change my paradigm and provide a happy home for my children."

PART TWO

Triumph Over Paradigm™

Introduction to the
Triumph Over Paradigm ™

The "Triumph Over Paradigm" is a dynamic model designed to aid teachers, parents, and children understand the relationship between thoughts, words and diet and how all three affect behavior.

With simplicity and effectiveness in mind, the paradigm incorporates a 'back to basics' approach to improving symptoms related to attention deficit disorders and disruptive behaviors.

The model is fueled by education and is driven by making informed decisions, then acting on them.

How the "Triumph Over Paradigm"
was developed

After being diagnosed with a hard-to-treat form of breast cancer, I had to make the decision whether to go with traditional treatment or an alternative treatment.

The first thing I did was to learn as much as I could about alternative healing. The alternative and natural health education I received fueled my desire to learn more. The more I learned, the more I realized an alternative course of healing was the right choice for me.

Before the diagnosis, I was very closed minded and almost non-approachable concerning anything to do with health. No one could get me to stop drinking my soda or eating a whole pie in one sitting. Taking supplements was the furthest thing from my mind.

It's amazing how a life threatening disease can change all that. Within days of starting my education, I adopted my new thinking.

At the same time, the words I spoke to myself, as well as the words I spoke to others, changed. I have always been a positive person and my words reflected that attitude. Yet, during this learning process, I discovered the true impact attitude has on healing.

I began to translate my positive attitude into words of encouragement. Words like; "I am healed" and "I can do this" and "I am capable".

My words became powerful. They helped to manifest courage and confidence, empowering me to continue on my healing journey.

With this newfound courage and self-confidence came self-discipline. No longer did I eat life-robbing foods that helped to weaken my immune system and drain my brain. My new diet included nourishing foods: fresh fruits and vegetables, nuts, seeds and grains. I eliminated all foods with preservatives, additives and food colorings.

To my pleasant surprise, symptoms of ADD and Tourette syndrome almost disappeared! For the first time ever, I was able to focus and complete one task at a time. My attention span increased, motor tics diminished, verbal outbursts of curse words stopped, and I felt grounded. I felt euphoric.

Adopting this healthy lifestyle became easy and a life choice. It wasn't just "mumbo jumbo". It was real and the results were undeniable.

My experience taught me a valuable lesson. When a person is faced with a difficult decision or put in a compromising, negative or life threatening situation, they have choices.

By choosing to become empowered through education, a person will know they are making the best and most informed decision possible. The decision is made from a position of confidence, not fear.

The illustration below demonstrates the components of the "Triumph Over Paradigm" and how they interact.

Triumph Over Paradigm™

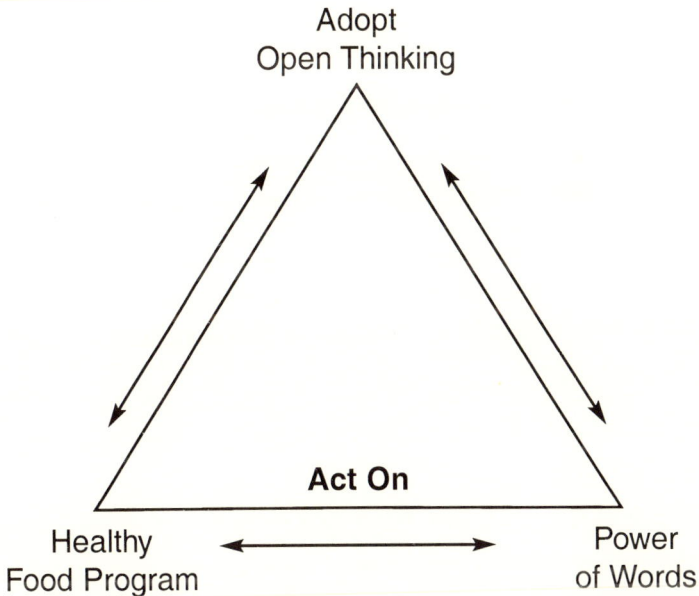

Adopt
Open Thinking

Act On

Healthy
Food Program

Power
of Words

chapter 5

Adopt Open Thinking

Before I explain how to adopt open thinking, it is important to understand what open thinking means. Open thinking simply means: opening your mind to possibilities you haven't considered before.

Open thinking begins with education. This section is devoted to education. The information presented is based on facts, research, and real life experiences. You will be exposed to the harmful effects of drugs used to treat attention deficit and disruptive disorders, as well as food additives that further aggravate the situation.

Various alternative and non-drug therapies are also presented including: herbal remedies, aromatherapy, BioSET allergy testing, CranioSacral therapy and effective attention grabbers.

Where to begin to adopt open thinking

My life experience and discussions with many other people have led me to believe the 1ˢᵗ step in adopting open thinking is to trust your own intuition. If you are a spiritual person, trust in God to bring you exactly the right information. The spirit will move you in the right direction. The reason I say this is: as you gather information from books, articles, the Internet, lectures,

59

seminars, other people, etc...the body of knowledge can become overwhelming. Therefore, you need to begin trusting yourself.

By doing this, you take back your own authority to make the decision as to which way you want to go, rather than leaving it in the hands of someone else to tell you what to do. Once you believe you have been presented with the right approach for your situation, then begin the sifting process.

Talk to people who have a personal success story. Speak to a child who is having success with a non-drug approach, as well as a child who is on prescription drugs. Attend support groups and parent groups to share your thoughts and get feedback. Parent and support groups may have alternative approaches you may not have considered. Attend seminars and lectures given by professionals in the alternative arena.

Remember Stephanie and her son Stephen. It took years of trying different drugs to treat Stephen's ADHD, before Stephanie tried something different. "The drugs were making him worse. I had to do something else so I went to the Internet to learn more about ADHD. All of a sudden, God presented me with an alternative approach. I was ready to change my thinking for Stephen's sake," she said.

Defining – Attention deficit and disruptive disorders & Tourette syndrome

Attention deficit and disruptive disorders

The exact cause of ADHD is unknown. Currently, it is believed that this disorder may be caused by a combination of factors including genetic, biological and environmental factors.

Other possible causes include:

- Alcohol, cigarette or other drugs used during pregnancy.
- Problems during pregnancy or delivery that cause injury to the brain.
- Infections that cause brain damage.
- Poor nutrition during a baby's first year of life.
- Lead poisoning.

Diagnosis

A diagnosis is made by comparing a child's behaviors with a description of the disorder as defined and accepted by experts in the field. Some of the behaviors include: fidgeting with limbs, squirms in seat, difficulty waiting his/her turn, easily distracted, difficulty sustaining attention to tasks and often talks excessively. None of the behaviors in themselves are abnormal. Most children display any of these behaviors and are not considered abnormal.

According to the diagnostic and Statistical Manual of Mental Disorders (DSM-IV), there are three basic categories for defining ADHD: Hyperactivity, impulsivity and problems with attention. The frequency, intensity or multiple behaviors are considered when making a diagnosis.

Tourette Syndrome

Tourette syndrome is a neurological disorder that is characterized by repeated involuntary movements and uncontrollable vocal (phonic) sounds called tics.

Tics can include eye blinking, neck jerking, tongue protrusions, shoulder shrugs, torso and limb movements, barks, cough, yelps etc. Tics can also include cursing (coprolalia). Some people with Tourette syndrome act out explicitly sexual gestures or displays (copropraxia).

The disorder is named for Dr. Georges Gilles de la Tourette, the pioneering French neurologist, who first described an 86-year-old French noblewoman with the condition in 1885.

The exact cause of Tourette syndrome is still unknown, but some of the theories include: Dr. Singer, professor of neurology at Johns Hopkins University School of Medicine. Dr. Singer suspects that a bacterial infection may trigger the condition in some genetically susceptible children. One bacterium under suspicion is streptococcus; commonly know as "strep."

Others suggest there is an abnormality in the gene(s) affecting the brain's metabolism of neurotransmitters. Neurotransmitters are the chemicals in the brain that carry signals from one nerve cell to another. These include dopamine, serotonin, and norepinephrine. At this time, there is no known medical cure.

Diagnosis

A Diagnosis of Tourette syndrome requires the presence of both motor and phonic for a period of at least 1 year.

Other disorders associated with Tourette syndrome

- Obsessive-compulsive behavior–the person feels that something must be done repeatedly

- Attention deficit disorder- where the person has difficulty concentrating and is easily distracted

- Learning disabilities-which include reading, writing, arithmetic, and perceptual difficulties

- Problems with impulse control-which can result in overly aggressive behaviors or socially inappropriate acts.

Dangers Of Prescription Drugs
prescribed for ADD, ADHD & Tourette syndrome

Not too long ago, I read one of the best books ever written about Ritalin and other drugs prescribed for ADD & ADHD. I was shocked by what I read. By the end of the book I felt well informed and empowered to share the information.

This outstanding book is entitled, "Talking Back To Ritalin, What doctors aren't telling you about stimulants for children", written by Peter R. Breggin, M.D.

Dr. Breggin is a psychiatrist and one of the world's foremost critics of biological psychiatry, including medication, and is a strong advocate for psychological and social human services. Dr. Breggin is in private practice in Bethesda, Maryland, where he also directs the International Center for the study of Psychiatry and Psychology. He teaches on the faculty of the Johns Hopkins University Department of Counseling.

The factual information is an eye opener for anyone affected directly or indirectly by ADD, ADHD and disruptive disorders. Dr. Breggin offers a new vision, so parents can make more informed decisions.

Every day millions of parents are faced with the difficult decision of whether or not to allow their children to be put on stimulant drugs. Most parents feel helpless and trust what their doctor is telling them.

Before you make this possible life-altering decision for your child (or for yourself) ask yourself and the doctor these questions:

- How safe is this drug?
- What are the side effects?
- What are the long-term effects?

Dr. Breggin has researched these questions extensively. He writes, "The debate about Ritalin and ADHD has been lopsided. Almost all the "scientific" information has come from doctors and groups who advocate drug treatment."

His book offers studies that correct this imbalance by providing facts doctors who prescribe the drugs will not even know. How could they? Doctors are so busy and don't have but a few minutes to spend with their patients. Let alone go home at the end of the day and read up on all of the different drugs they are prescribing.

The shocking truth begins in our homeland. America uses 90% of the world's Ritalin. What alarmed me most when reading Dr. Breggin's book, were the cases he cited of parents being pressured into putting their children on psychiatric drugs because their kids were being disruptive in school. Ritalin and other drugs have become the "norm" in our society. Parents have even been forced by the courts to give these drugs to their children.

The pressure is on

Dr Breggin writes: "In Atlanta, a psychiatrist tells Joey's mother that her difficult-to-control six-year-old will "turn out badly" if she doesn't put him on Ritalin. He has both the "hyperactive" and the "impulsive" forms of

ADHD. His brain is "hard wired" that way, the doctor explains.

The doctor says he could do a "brain scan" of Joey to show her the differences in her son's brain. Mom doesn't like to hear that there's something the matter with Joey but it is a relief to know it's not her fault. It sometimes takes the "patience of a saint" to deal with Joey. He's been difficult ever since the divorce two years ago."

Another case..."In Boise, Idaho, a father finds that single-parenthood is far more difficult than he ever imagined. His two pre-teen sons listen to him fairly well but they refuse to pay attention to anything that the babysitter tells them after school.

Both boys are "impulsive," their pediatrician explains, and could benefit from Ritalin. The doctor is sure that their problems are genetic and biochemical, and they will need Ritalin for the rest of their lives. Meanwhile, it would make Dad's life a lot easier, too, and keep the babysitter from quitting."

Dr. Breggin continues to share, "One of the saddest aspects of the ADHD/Ritalin movement is the unbridled willingness to tell children they have "broken brains," even in children's books. "Putting on the Brakes" (1991) is a book for young children by Patricia O. Quinn, a pediatrician, and Judith M. Stern, a teacher. The book begins by comparing a child to a sports car:

"Imagine a slick, hot, red sports car driving around a track. It's flying down the stretches, speeding around the curves, smooth, low to the road, the engine racing...BUT...it has no brakes. It can't stop when the driver wants to stop. It can't slow down to a safer speed. It may get off the track, or even crash! It will certainly have a hard time proving to everyone what it really can do. If you have attention deficit hyperactivity disorder (ADHD), you may be just like that racing car. You have a good engine (with lots of thinking power) and a good strong body, but NO BRAKES."

The authors display, "courtesy of Alan J. Zametkin, M.D.," misleading photographs of brain scans from Zametkin's 1991 publication. The child will learn from this misinformation that "the decreased brain activity shows up in these pictures in the darker areas" or "the brain may not have enough neurotransmitters to relay messages consistently."

What a dreadful thing to tell children about themselves. It is not even true! As Zametkin himself admits, the brain scans don't show anything abnormal. There's no way to tell the brain of a child labeled ADHD from the brain of a "normal" child."

No one has the right to tell a parent that his or her child will turn out badly. How does a psychiatrist who spends a few minutes with two pre-teenagers predict that they will have to be on drugs for the rest of their lives? He hasn't met the babysitter and hasn't evaluated her. Dad probably had no idea how the babysitter behaved when he left the house.

Dr. Breggin continues to write, "professionals and parents have joined in an unfortunate alliance to absolve themselves of any psychological, social, or spiritual responsibility for the child's well-being. Instead, they rely on diagnoses and drugs. This not only harms the child, it robs the professional and parents alike of the deeper satisfactions that come with understanding the child's situation and reaching out to fulfill the child's needs."

➤ What if your child was acting out because he was upset over the divorce? Would that warrant him being drugged? Are you a child of divorced parents? Were you drugged because you were upset or acting out? What if Joey was allergic to certain foods or chemicals? What if he was just lacking minerals or vitamins? What if...what if...what if? There are so many "what ifs" to explore before resorting to drugs.

Stimulants, including Ritalin (methylphenidate), are drugs most frequently prescribed for ADHD. The FDA-approved label for Ritalin contains a "WARNING" section. The warning includes: "Ritalin should not be used in children under six years, since safety and efficacy for this age group have not been established and sufficient data on safety and efficacy of long-term use of Ritalin in children are not yet available."

Stimulants can produce the very symptoms they are supposed to control like: hyperactivity, impulsivity, and inattention. When children become stimulated while taking the drug, parents and doctors may mistakenly believe the child's ADHD is getting worse!

They may even increase the stimulant – drug. Ritalin also has a contraindication warning on the official label. A Contraindication means that it should never be used under specific conditions. **Contraindications of Ritalin are: marked anxiety, tension and agitation.** Aren't these the very symptoms doctors are prescribing Ritalin for?

Can your child develop Tourette syndrome while taking Ritalin?

"The official label for Ritalin states that Ritalin is contraindicated in patients with motor tics or with a family history or diagnosis of Tourette syndrome." I had to read this section over and over again. Dr. Breggin continues, "Remember, a contraindication is an absolute prohibition against using the drug under the specified conditions."

These statements made me think about my own tics, which included all of the ones Dr. Breggin was mentioning like: facial twitches and grimaces, eye blinking, abnormal movements of feet, hands, arms and legs.

At this point in Dr. Breggin's book, I decided I had to verify these findings for myself. I started at a local drug store and asked the pharmacist if he had any literature on the side effects of Ritalin. He printed out two pages entitled, "Patient Drug Education." Under the heading, "Possible Side Effects" was seizures, involuntary muscle movements and change in mood or personality.

Surprisingly, it was not as specific as the side effects outlined by Dr. Breggin. If I were a parent with a child who had Tourette syndrome I might not have put two and two together, just by reading what the pharmacist gave me.

My curiosity got the best of me, so I purchased, "The Physicians Desk Reference, Pocket Guide to Prescription Drugs (PDR)", (at the same drug store) to read what side effects it listed. There it was in black and white. Under the heading, "Why should this drug not be prescribed? Anyone who suffers from tics (repeated, involuntary twitches or someone with a family history of Tourette syndrome (severe and multiple tics)."

At this point I was on fire...I needed more information. I went to the local library and sat down at the Medical Reference Table. I scanned the books hoping one would jump out at me, it did. The book is titled, "The Essential Guide to Prescription Drugs 2002.

I checked the index for Ritalin and anxiously turned to the page. It read, "The drug should not be taken if you have Tourette syndrome or experience tics while using it.

Precipitation of Tourette syndrome." This last comment meant that Tourette syndrome could become permanent!

I would not wish Tourette syndrome on anyone. If Tourette syndrome were a possible side effect of stimulant drugs like Ritalin and I were a parent who was thinking of putting my child on Ritalin or already have him or her on it, I would find an alternative approach!

Dr. Breggin sites a disturbing case of a child who developed Tourette syndrome: "Gerald Golden reported an irreversible case of Tourette's. After eight weeks on Ritalin, 10 mg twice a day, a nine-year-old boy developed explosive noises resembling a cough and multiple tic movements of his face, arms, and body. Even the use of Haldol (haloperidol) could not completely suppress the disorder, which apparently became permanent."

Just because the FDA approves a drug doesn't mean it's safe!

The FDA emphasizes that its stamp of approval doesn't mean that the drug is safe. Major side effects can show up months or even years after the drug's initial approval.

"Dr. Breggin writes, "Seldane, a widely used antihistamine, was being withdrawn after 12 years of use due to fatal cardiac arrhytmias. Another more widely used drug, the Novartis laxative called Ex-Lax, was recently withdrawn from the market. The FDA concluded that its principal ingredient, phenolphthalein, is a potential cancer risk."

Remember the big hoop-la over the recall of the wonder weight loss drug, "fen-phen?" I guess the magic wore off, as drug-induced abnormalities of heart valves were reported. Dr. Breggin informs his readers that these drugs are cousins of Ritalin and amphetamines!

I cannot begin to tell you how many hundreds of antacid tablets I chewed during my twenties. I was dependent on antihistamines for my chronic allergies and sinus attacks.

Each time I took an antihistamine the symptoms of Tourette syndrome became much worse. I should have worn a "whip-lash collar" during my twenties, due to the times I violently jerked my head backwards after taking antihistamines. I still have a tendency to do the same thing when I consume sugar, caffeine or alcohol!

Ritalin is compared to cocaine

"Cocaine, one of the most reinforcing and addictive of abused drugs, has pharmacological actions very similar to those for MPH (methylphenidate - Ritalin), one of the most commonly prescribed psychotropic medications for children in the United States" (Editorial comment in the Archives of General Psychiatry, 1995).

One final eye opening study: The American Psychiatric Association's Diagnostic and Statistical Manual of Mental Disorders IV, classifies Ritalin with the amphetamines, as a drug that has "amphetamine-like actions." It categorizes it together with amphetamine and methamphetamine ("speed"), as well as, cocaine for purposes of examining patterns of addiction, abuse, and toxicity.

The street name for Ritalin is R-ball or Vitamin R. It is one of the top prescription drugs stolen in the United States for recreational use.

Has anyone asked children how they feel about taking drugs?

In the midst of writing this book, I got to know Stephanie and her son, Stephen. Stephanie shared with me that her doctor never once asked Stephen how the drugs made him feel. I decided to ask Stephen myself and his response was, **"The pills make me feel really bad. It's like I get too much all at once."**

I thought it was very profound that Stephanie took one of Stephen's prescribed Ritalin pills and was shocked at how bad they made her feel. She told me, "I can't believe parents would let their kids take a drug they first didn't try themselves. Children are much smaller than parents. Just think how much worse they must feel?"

> ➤ For a number of reasons, children will almost always tell authority figures, such as doctors and parents, what they think the adults want to hear. Children have the need to be loved and approved of so, they may not tell the truth. They may consciously or unconsciously lie. They may want to avoid negative responses or punishment for not liking or not taking the prescribed drug.

Kids today must be very confused about the drug message. They are told, "Say no to drugs" but they are taking drugs. It is a mixed message. They are also being taught at an early age that drugs make it all better. Doesn't it make sense that as they grow up, they may become more likely to take a pill to make "it" better?

Earlier in the book, Stephanie shared with us that her doctor wanted to prescribe Paxil for Stephen and she told him absolutely not! Paxil's safety and effectiveness in children has not been established. Side effects include:

dizziness, diarrhea, drowsiness, nausea, nervousness, insomnia, tremor, agitation, anxiety, blurred vision, drugged feeling, twitching, vomiting and even more side effects.

Some drug companies do not apply for FDA approval for children, because once a drug is approved for adults for any therapeutic purpose, physicians are legally free to prescribe it for any age group.

A February 2000 study of 200,000 children coordinated by the University of Maryland, found a large increase in Ritalin, Prozac and Clonidine prescriptions in patients less then four years old! (The Essential Guide to Prescription Drugs 2002).

Why are doctors prescribing Ritalin to children under 6 years old? Don't they care or are they too busy to stay informed about the drugs they are prescribing?

Another shocking piece of information I came across pertaining to Ritalin, was also in the, "The Essential Guide to Prescription Drugs 2002." It stated: "Natural Diseases or Disorders may be activated by this drug." Latent Epilepsy was one of the natural diseases listed!

Another heading entitled, "Herbal medicines to avoid", named four herbs to avoid. These included: St Johns Wort, Guarana, Ma Huang and Kola. If a person takes any one of these herbs while taking Ritalin, unacceptable central nervous system stimulation may result. Being an herbalist, this makes perfect sense to me. There are certain herbs that do not mix with prescription drugs.

I wanted to learn more!

I couldn't turn the pages fast enough to see what was written about Haldol. Here is what I found.

Haloperidol (Haldol) is an antipsychotic tranquilizer. It's used to treat Tourette syndrome. The drug works by interfering with a nerve impulse transmitter (dopamine). This drug reduces anxiety and agitation, improves coherence and thinking and abolishes delusions and hallucinations.

That's odd; I stopped taking Haldol as a child because I felt like I was going to hallucinate. In the PDR Handbook, it listed hallucinations as a possible side effect!

I continued reading below the heading, "adverse effects–serious." It stated; nervous system reaction, rigidity of extremities, tremors, seizures, constant movement, facial grimacing, eye rolling, spasm neck muscles, latent epilepsy, glaucoma, diabetes.

Why is Haldol being prescribed for Tourette syndrome, when the effects of the drug can be the same as the symptoms it is prescribed to help?

This is precisely the situation that presents itself to parents everyday. We have to start using our brains. We are capable. First we, as a society, have to move beyond a place of complacency. Then we have to regain confidence in our ability to make good decisions.

MSG -Excitotoxins
Are they exciting brain cells to death?

MSG and excitotoxins, which you will learn about in this chapter, are among the worst food additives for children and adults with attention deficit and disruptive disorders. These chemicals are found in many processed foods.

The following information is presented in the book entitled, "Excitotoxins, the Taste That Kills", written by Dr. Russell L. Blaylock M.D.

Dr. Blaylock is a board-certified neurosurgeon, who completed his medical training at the Louisiana State University School of Medicine in New Orleans, Louisiana. Russell L. Blaylock, M.D., is a member of the Congress of Neurological Surgeons, the American Association of Neurological Surgeons and the American Nutritionist Association.

> Dr. Blaylock writes, "If you were to learn that these chemicals added to food could cause brain damage in you and your children, as well as future learning and emotional difficulties, what would you do?

> Suppose evidence was presented to you strongly suggesting that the artificial sweetener in diet soft drinks may cause brain tumors and that the number of brain tumors reported since the introduction of this artificial sweetener has risen dramatically?

Neuroscientists have labeled these chemical compounds as "excitotoxins". When neurons in the brain are exposed to these substances, they become very excited and fire impulses rapidly until they reach a state of extreme exhaustion.

Hours later, these neurons suddenly die, as if they were being excited to death. Unfortunately, these excitotoxins stimulate the taste cells in the tongue and greatly enhance the taste of foods."

History of MSG

"For thousands of years, Japanese cooks added an ingredient (made from sea weed) to their foods to enhance the flavor. During the last century, the active chemical in this taste-enhancing ingredient was isolated. This chemical is called monosodium glutamate (MSG).

After World War II, American food manufacturers were adding millions of pounds of MSG to processed foods each year. MSG was thought to be completely safe and many cookbooks even recommended adding it to their recipes. The amount of MSG added to foods has doubled every decade since the 1940's.

In 1957, two ophthalmologists, Lucas and Newhouse, tested MSG on infant mice to study eye disease. When they examined eye tissue of the mice, they discovered the MSG had destroyed all of the nerve cells in the inner layers of the retina, which are the visual receptor cells of the eye. Even after this alarming discovery, MSG continued to be added to foods.

Approximately ten years later, John W. Olney, MD, a neuroscientist, repeated the Lucas' and Newhouse experiment in infant mice. He found that not only was the MSG toxic to the retina, it was also toxic to the brain.

He discovered that specialized cells in a critical area of the mice's brain, the hypothalamus, were destroyed after a single dose of MSG.

You would think these alarming findings would have put a ban on MSG being added to foods, especially BABY foods. Still, food manufacturers continued to add MSG and hydrolyzed vegetable protein (a compound containing three excitotoxin additives and some MSG) to a variety of foods, including baby foods. The concentrations of MSG found in baby foods were equal to that used to create brain lesions in experimental animals.

Tests showed immature animals (babies) were found to be more vulnerable to the toxic effects of MSG than were older animals (adults).

Dr. Olney gave his testimony before a congressional committee and the food manufacturers agreed to remove MSG from baby foods...or did they? Instead of adding pure MSG, they added hydrolyzed vegetable protein."

What is hydrolyzed vegetable protein?

Hydrolyzed vegetable protein, also referred to as vegetable protein or plant protein is said to be a safe natural substance made from plants. Yes, it is made from vegetables, but the fact of the matter is that the vegetables used are unfit for sale to consumers. That means you!

The extraction process of hydrolysis involves boiling these vegetables in a vat of acid and then neutralizing them with caustic soda. A brown sludge that collects on top is then scraped off and allowed to dry. The end result is a brown powder, high in three known excitotoxins: glutamate, aspartate, and cystoic acid (converts in the body to cystcine – an excitotoxin).

These excitotoxins are then added directly to foods, or mixed with other ingredients and added to foods to enhance their flavor. Some neuroscientists believe that exposure to these powerful compounds early in life could cause developmental brain defects, **resulting in learning difficulties and behavioral problems or even violent behavior** as the child grows older.

There is growing evidence that excitotoxins play a significant role in a wide range of degenerative brain diseases in adults.

As it stands today, the word monosodium glutamate (MSG) is not required on food labels unless the product contains 100% pure MSG. For example: if broth is one of the ingredients in the soup, and the broth contains pure MSG, MSG does not have to be listed. If the broth is sold alone, it must appear on the label.

Aspartate and Aspartame

Aspartate (found in diet beverages and artificial sweeteners) is an acidic amino acid used by the brain as a neurotransmitter. At higher doses, it can injure or kill neurons and is then considered an excitotoxin.

Aspartame (NutraSweet) is about 200 times sweeter than sugar. It is an artificial sweetener prevalent in diet foods and found in the following products: Instant breakfasts, breath mints, cereals, sugar-free chewing gum, coffee beverages, frozen desserts, gelatin desserts, juice beverages, laxatives, milk drinks, soft drinks, tabletop sweeteners, instant teas and coffees, topping mixes, wine coolers, yogurt and even some multivitamins.

"Regardless of claims of the FDA, a significant number of people have reported suffering ill effects as a result of aspartame consumption: including headaches, mood swings, changes in vision, nausea and diarrhea, sleep disorder, memory loss and confusion and even convulsions. Aspartame appears to be especially dangerous for children" – Aspartame (NutraSweet): Is It Safe? by H.J. Roberts (The Charles Press, 1990). A complete list of MSG and excitotoxins are listed on page 94.

Pregnant mothers beware!

During pregnancy, the placenta barrier (designed to protect the baby) and the blood brain barrier (designed to protect the brain) can be penetrated by excitotoxins.

Dr. Blaylock points out, "During periods of fever or viral infections other barrier systems such as the blood-brain barrier can temporarily lose competence. The same must be true of the placental barrier.

It appears that the placental barrier, like the blood-brain barrier, is not an absolute barrier to the passage of excitotoxins. Some of the excitotoxins, such as cysteine, can easily pass through the placental barrier and damage the developing brain of the baby.

Cysteine compounds are present in hydrolyzed vegetable protein and are being added to some bread doughs. It has been proposed that exposure to excitotoxins (such as glutamate and aspartate) during fetal life may cause alterations in brain development that could later result in such serious brain disorders as autism, learning disorders, hyperactive behavior and possibly schizophrenia. One of the reasons it is so difficult to convince the FDA bureaucrats of the connection between MSG and delayed brain damage in humans is due to the fact that it may take years before clinical signs of neurological damage show up."

Coffee & Caffeine

I did research to learn more about caffeine and it's effects on the brain. Below are a few alarming excerpts I found, especially for unborn babies.

"The U.S. Food and Drug Administration published a warning in 1980 advising pregnant women to restrict or even eliminate consumption of coffee given the teratogenic effect (the ability to cause birth defects) observed in rodents." – review, Dr. Astrid Nehlig, 1994 journal of Neurotoxicology and Teratology.

"...it seems that early caffeine exposure, even at quite low doses, is able to induce a wide variety of neurochemcial changes. These deficits concern both constitutive material such as proteins, DNA and RNA, and functional material such a neurotransmitters and ions."

"Offspring of female rats exposed to 60 or 100 mg/kg caffeine in their drinking water throughout gestation have exhibited reduced learning capacities as adults in a novel environment. In an open field, these animals also spend less time grooming, playing, and touching new objects.

The authors concluded that the behavioral effects induced by prenatal caffeine exposure could be related to the "hyperactive" children syndrome." (Sinton, S.M. et. Al., 1981).

Lower birth weight after 300 mg caffeine intake

"It is during the last trimester of pregnancy that the greatest spurt on fetal growth occurs. The present test results suggest that daily caffeine intake of 300 mg or more can interfere with normal fetal growth. The observed, relatively small birth weight reductions may be of minor importance to a healthy full-term baby of acceptable weight, but may be of major clinical significance for a pre-term or small infant.

Although 300mg of caffeine intake represents approximately 2-3 cups of coffee, many people don't realize the amount of caffeine they can consume from other sources besides coffee."

Source - Dr. B. Watkinson and P.A. Fried, Carleton University, Ottawa, Ontario, Canada "Maternal Caffeine Use Before, During and After Pregnancy and Effects Upon Offspring" Neurobehavioral Toxicology and Teratology, Vol. 7:9-17, 1985

More on caffeine

• **Caffeine** – An odorless, white powder with a bitter taste that occurs naturally in coffee, cola, guarana pate, tea, and kola nuts. Caffeine is the number one psychoactive drug. It is a central nervous system, heart, and respiratory system stimulant. Caffeine can alter blood sugar release and cross the placental barrier. It can cause nervousness, insomnia, irregular heartbeat, noises in the ear, and in high doses, convulsions. It has been linked to spontaneous panic attacks in persons sensitive to caffeine. The Journal of the American Medical Association, December 22, 1993, stated of women who consume the amount of caffeine in one and a half to three cups of coffee a day, many nearly double their risk of miscarriage (A Consumer's Dictionary of Food Additives).

Caffeine can be found in coffee, tea, cola, cocoa, chocolate and many other sources. It is even in some medication. Caffeine is also dehydrating! It causes the body to excrete more water than it actually takes in. The result is less fluid than you started with. It can lead to constipation and bladder infections and can also wash out nutrients from the body.

Thoughts to ponder

• If caffeine is a psychoactive drug, then what are the side effects when a child is taking prescription drugs and caffeine at the same time?

• Are symptoms associated with attention deficit and disruptive behaviors heightened? Is the brain on stimulus overload?

• If caffeine is dehydrating and a child doesn't drink enough water, could his/her symptoms be signs of dehydration, not attention disorders?

The Food –Mood Connection

There is a food-mood connection between what we eat and how we think and act. Think for a moment about your own experience after eating certain foods. How do you feel after eating a plate of pasta or a few slices of pizza? Do you feel lethargic, lazy or can't keep your eyes open?

How about after eating sugar, drinking coffee or a soda with caffeine? Do you feel revved up, high on energy and then all of a sudden hit a low and become anxious or irritable? How about when you eat something with sugar or caffeine before going to bed? Do you have trouble sleeping? How about after having eating something with MSG, do you get a headache?

Food-mood relationship lies in the neurotransmitters of the brain. These chemical messengers relay thoughts and actions along trillions of neural pathways.

Since food affects neurotransmitter action and changes in neurotransmitters are responsible for changes in moods, then it makes sense that food does affect mood.

How carbohydrates and sugar affect mood

Carbohydrates - While conducting research for this book, I came across the website www.askdrsears.com

This well presented website was filled with simple common sense explanations of how food affects mood, especially carbohydrates and sugars. Most people have heard the word carbohydrates and know about sugar, but don't really understand how they affect the body and the mind. This connection is very interesting and important for parents to know, especially as they choose to shop more consciously.

The brains' fuel source is glucose, but where does glucose come from? The brain is a sugar hog, a carbo-craver, utilizing 20 percent of the body's carbohydrate supply. Yet, it's a smart hog, being selective about the type of sugars it craves and how it processes them. It prefers a nice steady supply.

When the brain receives a steady supply of sugar for fuel, it chugs along smoothly at a steady pace. But when the brain receives a surge of the wrong sugars, levels in behavior and learning become more erratic. Blood sugar levels depend on what kinds of food are coming into the body.

There are two types of carbohydrates – carbohydrates that calm and carbohydrates that excite. Complex carbohydrates like legumes, unrefined grains and fruits usually have a relaxing effect because they cause fewer blood sugar disturbances.

Carbohydrates that excite, like sugars found in frostings and soft drinks tend to cause more blood sugar disturbances. These increased blood sugar disturbances may result in a person feel high, then low, then moody and irritable.

Sugar – Unfortunately, many scientists still discount the relationship between sugar and behavior. I encourage you to become your own "scientist of common sense". Observe a child's or even your own behavior after eating foods with glucose, sucrose, dextrose and highly refined sugars in candy, syrups, packaged baked goods and table sugar.

These sugars enter the bloodstream quickly, reaching high levels in a short time. These sugars are used rapidly and when they are all used up, the blood sugar level plunges to a sugar low, or hypoglycemia. The low blood sugar triggers the release of adrenal hormones that squeeze stored sugar from the liver sending blood sugar levels back up.

This blood sugar roller coaster affects mood and concentration in some children and adults, leading to "sugar highs" and "sugar blues." The ups and downs of blood sugar and adrenal hormones can also stimulate neurotransmitter imbalance, causing the child to feel fidgety, irritable, inattentive and even sleepy.

The best sugars for the brain are complex carbohydrates or starches. Starches and fruit sugars (fructose) do not cause the roller-coaster mood swings that the junk sugars do.

The molecule in complex carbohydrates is long, so it takes longer for the intestines to break them down into the simple sugars the body can use. Thus, they provide a time-release source of steady energy rather than a sudden surge followed by a sudden drop.

The rate at which sugar from a particular food enters brain cells and other cells of the body is called the "glycemic index" (GI) of a particular food.

Foods with a high glycemic index stimulate the pancreas to secrete a lot of insulin, which causes the sugar to quickly empty from the blood into the cells; this produces the ups and downs of low sugar and the roller coaster behavior that goes with them.

Foods with a low glycemic index do not push the pancreas to secrete so much insulin, so the blood sugar tends to be steadier. Feeding your child carbohydrate foods with a low glycemic index, is one way of helping them control their behavior and performance in school or at play.

➢ Brain friendly carbohydrates include: Fresh fruits, vegetables, beans (legumes), rice, oatmeal, whole grain cereals (without sugar) and yogurt (without fruit at the bottom).

➢ Encourage children to eat more fruit rather than drinking more juice. Whole fruit has a lower glycemic index than juice. By real juice instead of juice from concentrate or worse, juice drinks or juice flavored drinks (very little real juice and lots of sugars and flavorings). To dilute the sugar in juice add water or squeeze fresh lemon into it.

➢ Eating carbohydrates high on the glycemic index along with a fat or fiber can slow down the absorption into the bloodstream.

➢ Foods with a high glycemic index like juice, candy or dessert are best consumed with or after a meal, because the company of other foods slows the entry of sugar into the bloodstream and the brain.

➢ Teach children not to indulge in highly sweetened snacks between meals. It may hinder learning and increase disruptive behavior. Suggest eating an apple or some raw nuts and seeds.

The Constipation - Mood Connection

The following topic is very embarrassing for most people to address, so I will address it. Constipation has always been an issue for me. For most of my life I did not have regular bowel movements. A regular bowel movement is one to two times a day. I constantly suffered stomach problems constantly and stuffed as many flavored antacids in my mouth at a time as would fit. It wasn't until I changed my diet that I began having two bowel movements a day.

Think about this gross thought: If a person eats three meals a day and snacks in-between, but only has one bowel movement a day, or worse every other day, what happens to the waste that doesn't come out? Where does it go? Does it just magically disappear? No, it doesn't.

Over time, the bowel walls become encrusted, causing toxic build up in the colon. It interferes with vital nutrients being absorbed through the intestinal walls and channeled to where they are needed. If the toxicity level gets high enough, the blood capillaries lining the intestinal walls absorb these toxins into the bloodstream. They eventually invade and pollute the organs and cells.

After reading this information, isn't it possible that constipation could contribute to symptoms of attention and disruptive behaviors? The following true stories will help you to think about the correlation between constipation and moods.

Just a few months ago, I met a woman and told her I was writing a book. We began sharing stories and somehow the subject of constipation came up. She told me about the time her young child was crying all the time and throwing fits. She took her child to the doctor, but the doctor didn't know what was wrong. After numerous attempts at solving the problem with prescription drugs, the mother took the child to see a naturopathic doctor. Within minutes of examining the child, he diagnosed the child as being severely constipated.

After an enema and the addition of an herbal bowel improvement formula, her son was no longer crying or throwing fits.

Another true story involves a teenage girl who had only one bowel movement every two weeks. Her mother told me that her daughter was on anti-depressants because she isolated herself and wouldn't socialize. The mother began to learn about diet and constipating foods. Both the mother and daughter began to drink more water and stopped eating white bread, meat and cheese. Within one month, her daughter began having regular bowel movements and weaned off anti-depressants.

NOTE: Is your child having at least one or two bowel movements a day? If not, it's a sensitive subject that needs addressing. It's important to encourage young children to go to the bathroom and not wait until they get home. Waiting gives them the message that it is not good to go to the bathroom in public places. The problem with waiting is, by the time a child gets home, they may not have to go anymore. This sets a child up to suffer the consequences of constipation later in life.

Simple natural remedies for constipation

- 8oz of warm water with the juice of one lemon, first thing in the morning.

- 2-3 tablespoons of ground flaxseeds in juice or water, before bedtime or first thing in the morning.

Crash Course
Reading Labels 101

Learning to recognize harmful ingredients is your first line of defense in achieving positive results with ADD, ADHD and Tourette syndrome.

Recall when Stephanie shared with us that she taught her son Stephen, who was diagnosed with ADHD, how to read labels to identify what he could and couldn't have? After just a few visits to the grocery store, Stephen voluntarily and eagerly reads labels.

The following items are popular foods and beverages found in the grocery store (brand names are not disclosed). The ingredients listed below appear exactly as they do on the label of the item. I have bolded the ingredients in question (not all ingredients are listed).

On the next page, you will find the descriptions of each of the ingredients and additives in question. Don't just stop here, look up the ingredients and additives for yourself in the, "A Consumer's Dictionary" and on the Internet.

• <u>CANNED SOUP</u>

Chicken stock, rice, cooked chicken meat, water, carrots, salt, **monosodium glutamate**, celery, **chicken flavor**, onion powder, **spice extract**, disodium inosinate, disodium guanylate, soy protein isolate, **sodium phosphates**, lactic acid, **flavoring**, beta carotene for color.

This particular brand of soup has MSG and possibly three other forms of excitotoxins – chicken flavor, spice extract and flavoring. What are sodium phosphates doing in soup?

• ENERGY DRINKS

Energy drink #1 - Carbonated water, **sucrose**, **glucose**, sodium citrate, taurine, glucurono-lactone, **caffeine**, inositol, niacinamade, calcium pantothenate, pyrdoxine HCL, vitamin B12, **artificial flavors**, **colors**.

Energy drink #2 – Carbonated water, **high fructose corn syrup**, **glucose**, taurine, citric and ascorbic acid, **panax ginseng (root)**, **natural flavors**, **caffeine**, gingko biloba (leaf), gum arabic, **guarana extract**, niacinamide, turmeric color, ester gum, riboflavin, pyridoxine hydrochloride, cyanobalamin.

Drink #1 has two forms of sugar, caffeine, artificial flavors and colors – sure they add some herbs to the drink but it doesn't void the harmful effects of the other ingredients.

Drink #2 is very dangerous for children and adults with attention disorders and Tourette syndrome. It is loaded with stimulants and possibly an excitotoxin.

• FLAVORED POTATO CHIPS

Potatoes, corn and/or cottonseed oil, salt, maltodextrin, sugar, dextrose, brown sugar, partially hydrogenated soybean oil, onion powder, **monosodium glutamate**, **spices**, corn syrup solids, tomato powder, **artificial colors (including yellow 5 lake, yellow 6 lake, blue 2 lake, red 40, yellow 5, blue 1)**, **autolyzed yeast extract**, garlic,

sodium caseinate, **carrageenan**, disodium inosinate, disodium guanylate, acetic acid.

This particular potato chip is a toxic mix of MSG, sugar and food colorings. Most of these ingredients are added to the flavoring.

• SALAD DRESSING

Soybean oil, water, nonfat buttermilk, **high fructose corn syrup**, distilled vinegar, **monosodium glutamate**, **spices**, **polysorbate 60**, **natural flavors**, disodium inosinate and disodium guanylate.

This salad dressing has sugar, MSG and possibly two more forms of excitotoxins. Look up polysorbate 60 – what the heck is it doing in salad dressing?

• CHEESE SPREAD

Comes in a can - Cheddar cheese, disodium phosphate, lactic acid, salt, **autolyzed yeast extract (contains glutamate), carrageenan**, sorbic acid.

This popular cheese spread contains MSG!

• CANDY

A form of gummy candy – **Corn syrup, sugar**, gelatin, water, lactic and fumaric and citric acids (for tartness), sorbitol, natural and **artificial flavors, artificial color (includes red 40, yellow 5, yellow 6, blue 1)**.

A form of milk chocolate candy – Milk chocolate, dextrose, **maltodextrin, sugar, artificial flavors, carnuba wax, blue 1, blue1 lake, blue 2 lake, carmine color, red 40, red 40 lake**, titanium dioxide, **yellow 5, yellow 5 lake, yellow 6 lake.**

The ingredients in both of these candies can cause a child to fly through the roof. They are filled with chemicals – notice all of the colorings. These candies should be limited or avoided completely by children with attention disorders and Tourette syndrome.

NOTE: Unfortunately, many medical professionals still do not understand the relationship between these harmful food additives and attention and behavior disorders. They are unfamiliar with these additives. It is up to you to make this important connection by observing your child's behavior, after consuming foods and beverages containing these additives.

Try drinking one of these energy drinks yourself to see how it affects you. Try some of these chemically loaded candies before giving it to your child. Remember, if your child is on medication, he or she may have a much more heightened reaction to these additives than you do, if you are not taking the same medication.

Foods to Avoid

- **Instant soups** with MSG and excitotoxins
- **Canned soups** with added MSG and excitotoxins
- **Chips with flavoring added** or any flavored snacks
- **Instant puddings and Jell-O**
- **Diet and low fat foods** – check label for artificial sweeteners, aspartate and aspartame
- **Instant breakfast toaster meals**
- **Frozen oriental foods** with MSG and excitotoxins
- **Prepackaged luncheon meats**
- **Prepackaged complete lunch meals**
- **Artificial meats**
- **Some salad dressings** check labels
- **Foods with the first three ingredients being some form of sugar: corn syrup, sugar and ending in "ose" Fructose is ok**
- **Flavored coffee creamers**
- **Candy! Especially flavored candy** (check for food colorings and excitotoxins)

***Beverages with added caffeine, ginseng, ma huang, guarana, kola** *and/or* **colorings** – (see page 95, 96, 97)

To avoid bad dreams or a restless sleep, avoid eating or drinking anything containing food coloring, MSG or caffeine before bedtime (check labels on desserts as well).

Hidden Sources of MSG

- Monosodium Glutamate
- Hydrolyzed Vegetable Protein
- Hydrolyzed Protein
- Hydrolyzed Plant Protein
- Plant Protein Extract
- Autolyzed Yeast
- Hydrolyzed Oat Flour
- Sodium Caseinate
- Calcium Caseinate
- Yeast Extract
- Textured Protein

Additives that Frequently Contain MSG

- Malt Extract
- Bouillon
- Stock Flavoring
- Natural Beef
- Seasoning
- Broth
- Natural Flavoring
- Chicken Flavoring
- Malt Flavoring
- Spices

They are often used in

- Soups, sauces, gravy mixes, low fat & diet foods, instant foods, salad dressings and oriental foods. I have found it in many other foods, as well.

Food Additives

The following information was taken from the book, "A Consumers Dictionary Of Food Additives", written by Ruth Winter, M.S. This book is handy to have with you while grocery shopping.

• **Caffeine** – An odorless, white powder with a bitter taste that occurs naturally in coffee, cola, guarana pate, tea, and kola nuts. <u>Caffeine is the number one psychoactive drug</u>. It is a central nervous system, heart, and respiratory system stimulant. Caffeine can alter blood sugar release and <u>cross the placental barrier</u>. It can cause nervousness, insomnia, irregular heartbeat, noises in the ear, and in high doses, convulsions. It has been linked to spontaneous panic attacks in persons sensitive to caffeine. The Journal of the American Medical Association, December 22, 1993, said that women who consume the amount of caffeine in one and a half to three cups of coffee a day many nearly <u>double their risk of miscarriage</u>.

• **MSG** – Monosodium Glutamate is used to intensify spice flavorings in meats, condiments, pickles, soups, candy, and baked goods. Believed to be responsible for "Chinese-restaurant syndrome" in which diners suffer from chest pain, headaches, and numbness after eating a Chinese meal. Causes brain damage in young rodents and brain damage effects in rats, rabbits, chicks, and monkeys. <u>Depression, irritability and other mood changes have been reported.</u>

• **Kola** – Kola nut extract – guru nut. A natural extract from the brownish seed produced by trees in Africa, the West Indies and Brazil. <u>Contains caffeine.</u>

• **Ma Huang** – Ephedra, acts as a decongestant and stimulates the central nervous system. Warning: <u>Do not use ephedra products if you are under the age of 18</u>. Consult a doctor before using ephedra if you have depression or psychiatric condition or taking a prescription drug. <u>Individuals who consume caffeine with these products may experience serious adverse health effects</u> - source www.botanical.com

• **Guarana** – A crystallizable principle, called guaranine, identical with caffeine. Guarana is a nervine, tonic and has a slightly narcotic stimulant. The Brazilian miners drink this constantly and believe it to be a preventive of many diseases. It has the same chemical composition as caffeine, theine and cocaine, and the same physiological action – source www.botanical.com

• **Polysorbate 60 and Polysorbate 80** – Both are emulsifiers that have been associated with the <u>contaminant 1,4 dioxane, known to cause cancer in animals</u>. Polysorbate 60 is added to chocolate coatings, found in frozen and gelatin desserts, cakes, cake mixes, doughnuts, and artificial chocolate coatings, nondairy whipped cream and creamers, salad dressings made without eggs and vitamin supplements. Polysorbate 80 is used in baby lotions, cold creams, deodorants, suntan lotions, etc.

• **Hormones** – A hormone is a chemical produced by a gland and secreted into the bloodstream, affecting the function of distant cells or organs. U.S. beef producers have been using growth hormones, powerful chemicals from the pituitary gland at the base of the brain, to increase the weight of cattle from 10 to 2 percent for the same amount of feed. Diethylstilbestrol, another hormone, an estrogen was used by beef and poultry producers to increase the weight of meat, for which they are paid by the pound.

The FDA has tried to ban diethylstilbestrol for that purpose because it <u>has been shown to be carcinogenic</u>, but spot checks have shown that it is still present in some meat and poultry product. Hormones are still being used in feed and by implantation in cattle, chickens, and turkeys, as you can determine by checking listings, including those for estradiol, mibolerone, testosterone propionate, and trenbolone.

• **Propylene Glycol** – 1,2-Propanediol, used in confectionery, chocolate products, ice cream emulsifiers, shredded coconut, beverages, baked goods, toppings, icings, and meat products to prevent discoloration during storage. Large doses in animals have reported to cause central nervous system depression.

• **Nitrites** – Potassium and Sodium. Potassium nitrite is used as a color fixative in the cured-meat business. Sodium nitrite has the peculiar ability to react chemically with processed meats to convey tanginess to the palate. It is used as a color fixative in cured meats, bacon, bologna, frankfurters, deviled ham, meat spread, spiced ham, Vienna sausages, smoke-cured tuna fish products and in smoke-cured shad and salmon. Nitrite combines with natural stomach and food chemical to create nitrosamines, powerful cancer-causing agents. If you must eat nitrite-laced meats, include a food or drink high in vitamin C at the same time – orange juice, grapefruit juice, cranberry juice or lettuce.

• **Coal Tar** - Used in adhesives, insecticides, woodworking, preservation of food, synthetic flavors, and dyes to make colors used in cosmetics, including hair dyes. Derived from bituminous coal. The main concern about coal-tar derivatives is that they cause cancer in animals, but they are also frequent sources of allergic reactions, particularly skin rashes and hives.

• **Sodium Phosphate** – Buffer and effervescent used in the manufacture of nail enamels and detergents.

• **BHT** - Butylated Hydroxytoluene, is a preservative and antioxidant added to many foods. Can cause allergic reactions.

The Select Committee of the American Societies for Experimental biology, which advises the FDA on food additives, recommended further studies to determine "the effects of BHT at levels now present in foods under conditions where steroid hormones or oral contraceptives are being ingested. They said the possibility that BHT <u>may convert other ingested substances into toxic or cancer-casing agents</u> should be investigated." BHT is prohibited as a food additive in England.

• **BHA** – Butylated Hydroxyanisole, is a preservative and antioxidant in many products including: beverages, ice cream, ices, candy, baked goods, chewing gum, gelatin desserts, soup bases, potatoes, dry breakfast cereals, and more. <u>Can cause allergic reactions.</u>

• **Hickory Smoke Condesate (HSG)** – A food flavoring. Available data have suggested that this <u>additive has tumor-initiating and –promoting potential.</u>

• **High Fructose Corn Syrup** – Corn sugar (dextrose) that has been treated with enzymes to make it sweeter.

• **Artificial Ingredients** – Cannot be duplicated in nature! Not real.

• **Artificial Colors** – The information is much too long to give you in this book. Look this one up for yourself. Many artificial colors used in food are derived from coal tar (see coal tar). Here are a few excerpts: FD and C Red No. 40 – many American scientists feel that the safety of Red No. 40 is far from established, particularly because all the tests were conducted by the manufacturer, and therefore, the dye should not have received a permanent safety rating. <u>The National Cancer Institute reported that p-credine, achemical used in the preparation of Red No. 40, was carcinogenic in animals.</u>

FD and C Yellow No. 5 – A coal tar derivative, used in prepared breakfast cereals, imitation strawberry jelly, bottled soft drinks, gelatin desserts, ice cream, sherbets, dry drink powders, candy, puddings, etc. It is estimated that half of the aspirin-sensitive people plus 47,000 to 90,000 others in the nation are sensitive to this dye. Aspirin sensitive patients have been reported to develop life-threatening asthmatic symptoms upon ingestion of Yellow No. 5.

WARNING: Do not mix energy drinks containing caffeine, guarana, ginseng, ma huang or kola with medication prescribed for ADD, ADHD and Tourette syndrome. Check with your doctor. These drinks are heavy stimulants and should not be mixed with any medications, not even over the counter medications.

Non-Drug Approaches

Hooray! Good news! More and more people are seeking safer alternatives to drugs. The following alternative approaches are ones I have personally used.

While exploring alternative therapies, keep in mind that it wasn't too long ago chiropractors were considered "Quacks" by the medical community. Today chiropractic care is among the respected forms of health care. The same is true for naturopathic doctors.

For over five thousand years, the Chinese culture has treated patients with herbs and acupuncture. Over the past ten years, these treatments have continued to gain acceptance. The medical profession has even given some credence to the healing power of prayer.

Times are changing. More and more people are no longer satisfied with the notion that drugs are the cure all for everything and are seeking more natural therapies. We must consider the premise medicine was built on. The Hippocratic oath states, "First, Do No Harm."

Natural health focuses on cleansing, building, supporting and strengthening the body. When the body is strengthened, it is able to fight disease and infection. For herbal remedies to be optimally effective, one must stop doing the things causing the disease or disorder in the first place.

Herbal Remedies

Ideally, for herbal remedies to be completely effective, attention to the whole body is important. Herbs can be thought of as concentrated foods that nourish the body and the brain. It may not be an overnight quick fix, like society is accustomed to, however, the reward is worth the effort put in over time.

Just as with drugs, herbal dosages may vary from person to person. It is beneficial to work with a qualified herbalist, naturopathic doctor or naturopathic medical doctor.

Brain Boosting Vitamins and Minerals

Vitamins and minerals are essential for a healthy immune system, tissue growth and conversion of food into energy. They can also have a strong influence on moods! The American diet of today is lacking the nutrients vital to supplying the brain with proper nutrition.

In a recent article written by Ronald Kotulak of the Chicago Tribune, it seems the AMA is agreeing that we really do need multivitamins. The article reads, "Reversing a long-standing anti-vitamin policy, the Journal of the American Medical Association today is advising all adults to take at least one multivitamin pill each day.

Scientists' understanding of the benefits of vitamins has rapidly advanced and it now appears that people who get enough vitamins may be able to prevent such common chronic illnesses as cancer, heart disease and osteoporosis, according to Dr. Robert H. Fletcher and Kathleen M. Fairfield of Harvard University."

A gradual depletion of essential nutrients, often hard to detect, can result in depression, anxiety, irritability, loss of appetite, sleepiness or insomnia.

When people begin to feed their brains nutrition and drink more water, they become more alert and aware. The following is a list of helpful brain boosters.

- **Essential Fatty Acids** - help to improve general brain functioning and restore memory, while aiding in the transmission of nerve impulses.

- **Vitamin C** - is required by the brain to make neurotransmitters.

- **Vitamin B12** - is vital to maintaining healthy myelin sheath, the tissue that covers and insulates nerve tissue.

- **Vitamin B6** - deficiency causes hyper-irritability and fatigue.

- **Folic Acid** - deficiency seems to affect neurotransmitter function, resulting in symptoms of depression.

- **Zinc** - deficiency has been linked to behavior problems including ADD. Zinc dosage must be monitored for weight and condition.

- **Magnesium** - deficiency has been associated with hyper activity and inattention.

Specific herbs that have been helpful with ADD, ADHD and Tourette syndrome:

• **Ginkgo biloba** - increases blood flow to the brain resulting in mental clarity, increased concentration and focus. It has the ability to squeeze through even the narrowest of blood vessels to increase the supply of oxygen to the heart, brain, and all other body parts. It is known as the "smart herb".

• **Valerian root** - is a natural sedative and relaxant, which calms often within minutes.

• **Passionflower** - acts as a gentle sedative. Helpful for anxiety, hyperactivity, and stress-related disorders.

• **Scullcap herb** - aids sleep, improves circulation, good for anxiety, hyperactivity, nervous disorders and spasms.

• **Catnip** - is good for anxiety, colds flu, inflammation, pain and stress.

• **Hops** - is good for anxiety, hyperactivity, insomnia, nervousness and restlessness.

• **Blue Cohosh** - relieves muscle spasms and is useful for memory problems and nervous disorders.

Other herbs include: Wild Yam, Milky Oats, Chamomile and Lobelia.

A naturopathic doctor, naturopathic medical doctor, qualified herbalist or chiropractor trained in herbal medicine can help with herbal combinations for the brain (possibly even a psychiatrist trained in herbal medicine).

Aromatherapy

This pleasant and non-invasive form of healing and relaxation uses aromatic essences of plant extracts called essential oils, for healing and relaxation.

Essential oils can be applied directly on the body, indirectly to a pillow or added to bath water. There are many more applications as well as varieties of essential oils. The best way to become familiar with the healing qualities of essential oils is to read a book or search the Internet.

A few essential oils that have a calming effect are:

- **Lavender** - essential oil used to instantly balance the central nervous system. It has a tranquilizing effect resulting in calmness.

- **Peppermint** - energizes with its strong menthol content. Helps to clear the mind and stabilize the emotions. It has the ability to create a feeling of calm vitality.

BioSET Allergy Elimination

Food and environmental sensitivities and allergies are increasing for many reasons. It is estimated that there are over 50,000 chemicals in our air, food and water that are not naturally occurring (these chemicals are not meant to be there).

As a result of poorly digested foods, polluted air and water, emotional stress, environmental toxins, metabolic wastes, etc., our bodies become toxic. The body normally tries to eliminate these toxins as best it can, but eventually it could become over burdened.

That's when we begin experiencing symptoms and disease. Conventional medicine believes that symptoms and disease should be controlled and suppressed usually with drugs.

BioSET is a breakthrough treatment that uses the latest state-of-the-art energetic medicine, chiropractic techniques and acupressure to permanently desensitize people to food and environmental allergies. The system assists in healing and building the body in strength and vitality. BioSET was developed by Dr. Ellen Cutler in 1997.

Kyle D. Christensen, a Chiropractor, Naturopath and Herbalist practicing in Citrus Heights, California at the *Well Being Health Center,* has been using BioSET Allergy Elimination in his practice for many years with positive results.

Dr. Christensen shares, "Often parents will comment that they have a new child – one that isn't hyper, mean and angry anymore. Common allergies found with these children are: food colorings, food additives (MSG, preservatives, etc.), sugar, amino acids, phenolics, fatty acids, various chemicals and environmental allergies."

Our immune systems have become weakened due to constant exposure to environmental pollutants, poisons, chemicals, food and water. We then begin to develop allergies to substances that should be considered normal. When the body reacts with symptoms of allergies, energy pathways in the body known as "meridian" can become blocked.

Any time there are energy blockages in the body, health problems result. Energetic blockage, cellular congestion and toxicity can result in symptoms such as: aches, pains in the body, sore throats, fevers, chills, painful lymph nodes, weakness, extreme fatigue, headaches, sleep disturbance, irritability, confusion, depression, forgetfulness, burning sensations in the body, frequent urination, crying spells, sores in mouth, indigestion, bloating, water retention and suicidal behavior.

BioSET practitioners use chiropractic manipulation techniques to stimulate points (often referred to as acupuncture points) that are connected to the meridians. If a blockage affects a certain organ, the practitioner stimulates acupuncture points along the spine that are connected to that organ by autonomic nerve impulses.

For example: To treat wheat allergy, the practitioner stimulates acupuncture points along the spine related to the lungs, while the person holds a vial containing the wheat allergen. After this treatment is completed, the person is no longer sensitive to wheat. This technique can be effectively used with any allergen, sensitivity or stressor to the body. BioSET treatments have been very effective with ADD and behavioral disorders.

To learn more about BioSET Allergy Elimination, visit: www.westernbotanicals.com/wellbeing.

CranioSacral Therapy

CranioSacral therapy is a relaxing, light touch healing modality, which monitors the cranial rhythms produced by the cerebrospinal fluid that surrounds and flows through the brain and spinal cord.

An imbalance in the CranioSacral system could play a role in causing behavior problems such as ADD, ADHD and learning disabilities.

By using a very gentle touch, the therapist is able to balance the flow of the cerebrospinal fluid, which encourages the body when it is ready, to release these restrictions and return it to a more naturally balanced and relaxed state. This is when physical and/or emotional healing can take place.

Research and clinical experience suggest that at least 50% of ADD and other learning disabilities are related to structural dysfunctions as a result of birth trauma and are amenable to correction through the proper application of CranioSacral therapy. When these corrections are made, the results are usually permanent.

Seek someone who has experience working with children. Most CranioSacral practitioners are massage therapists, but many physical therapists, chiropractors and medical doctors are trained and certified in this form of gentle manipulation.

My personal experience with CranioSacral therapy

A few years ago, I decided to see what CranioSacral therapy was all about and if it could help me with Tourctte syndrome. My therapist's were two female massage therapists trained at the Upledger Institute. The

107

therapists had me lay on my back (fully clothed) on a massage table. One of the therapist's began gently working on my head and neck, while the other worked on different parts of my body. They explained that what they were doing was facilitating my body to release blocked energy. The experience was amazing. I could actually feel the areas release and relax. Not once did I feel pain or discomfort.

The therapist working on my head and neck couldn't believe how twisted the inside of my neck felt. She explained how there was a blockage of the fluid in my neck and down my spine.

What she said made sense because one of my Tourette symptoms (tics) is jerking my neck forcefully to the side. Even before my first experience with CranialSacral therapy, I felt as if my neck was all twisted up. I didn't reveal this information to either of the therapists, until the end of the session.

When the therapist working on my neck finished, I felt like I had a brand new neck. My entire body felt open, as if everything was flowing perfectly. I even felt taller.

I thought it was my imagination, but it wasn't. The therapist explained how she felt that my neck was jammed into my skull. It was possible that it happened during my birth. As soon as I got home, my husband measured my height. I was ½" taller! I continue to have CranioSacral sessions as often as possible.

Attention Grabbers

The following "attention grabbers" for small children are highly effective and can be used by both parents and teachers to help children become more focused and calm.

Blowing Up Balloons - "Take a deep breath and see yourself filling up just as if you were a balloon...then slowly let the air out of the balloon." Repeat two or more times.

This is a very effective stress release for children and adults. Use your imagination or let the children use their imagination as to what they are blowing up. Ask them questions afterwards. For example: "How did you feel, after filling yourself up like a balloon and then letting out the air?"

The Honey Jar - "Imagine that you're moving in a jar of honey. You need to move very slowly."

This is a good exercise to do with a child at home and/or at school. First, do it with the child and then have them do it on their own. Walk the length of a room. Ask for feedback such as, how they felt walking through honey.

Robot/Rag Doll - "Make your body as stiff as a robot's for several seconds, then make it as limp as a rag doll's for several seconds." Repeat 3 times or more. Again, ask for feedback.

The Cat - "Lying face down on the floor, stretch arms, legs, arch the back and yawn, just like a cat." Repeat two or more times.

The Desk Bureau – Is a child's very own cubicle (office). Make a three-sided wall by cutting cardboard and taping it together. This is very effective because it eliminates distractions. Perfect for a child who does homework in their bedroom.

The Listening Chair – Is effective in a classroom setting and in a home setting. A chair designated for listening only, no talking.

Conditioning - **Do not** let ADD, ADHD or Tourette syndrome be an excuse for a child not to finish what they start. If necessary, help a child finish one task at a time by standing beside them, while they finish. Give them a time goal to complete a task. Tell them, "I am confident you can do it" or "I will help you learn to finish what you start."

Children and adults with attention deficit problems must be conditioned to complete tasks. Their tendency is to start something, then go on to something else. I know this from my personal experience with ADD and Tourette syndrome.

In the past I would begin doing the dishes, then half way through I would start on something else. Within minutes, I was back in the kitchen doing the dishes. Still today, I have to make a conscious effort to complete a task once I begin.

It takes self-discipline and practice. It is much easier if you begin conditioning and teaching your children self-discipline at an early age.

Adopt Open Thinking
Quick Guide

- Open your mind to consider alternatives.

- Get at least two opinions about your situation.

- Once a doctor or psychiatrist has made a diagnosis and recommends a prescription drug, look up the drug, it's side effects, and long term effects.

- Seek the opinion of a naturopathic medical doctor, naturopathic doctor or a qualified herbalist.

Education and Resources

- THE PDR Pocket Guide To Prescription Drugs (Physician's Desk Reference) available at bookstores

- The Essential Guide To Prescription Drugs 2002 by James J. Rybachki, Pharm. D available in bookstores and libraries

- On the Internet at **www.PDR.NET**

- Talking Back To Ritalin, by Peter R. Breggin, M.D.

- Excitotoxins, The Taste That Kills, by Russell L. Blaylock, M.D.

- Tourette Syndrome Association, Inc. 42-40 Bell Boulevard Bayside, New York 11361-286 718-224-2999 or 1-888-486-8738

- Attention Deficit Disorder Association 1788 Second Street, Suite 200, Highland Park, IL 60035 1-847-432-ADDA or E-mail: mail@add.org

chapter 6

Manifesting Power Of Words

The power of words is manifested in:

- What you say
- What you don't say
- How you receive what is said to you
- How you respond to what is said to you

Recently, I attended a women's group monthly gathering. The featured speaker was Nancy Harkins, an international motivational speaker, trainer, facilitator and consultant. The talk that she delivered was on communication.

Her message was: *YOUR WORDS HAVE POWER.* The words you use when speaking to and about yourself and to and about another person have power, so choose your words very carefully.

Nancy revealed a simple process of how to choose our words, in order to give life to any given situation. As I listened to Nancy deliver her message with authority and vibrancy, I knew teachers, parents and children would benefit from her practical wisdom.

I invited Nancy to my home for a personal interview. I wanted to know how she suggests the power of words can help teachers and parents speak encouragement into the lives of children. My interview began by asking Nancy to explain how "power" manifests through our

113

words. Nancy Harkins' reply to my question resulted in the personalized seminar that follows:

Power in words is manifested in what and who we are. For example: If you repeatedly say to yourself, "I am stupid, I am sick, I am angry, I am tired", the end result is the manifestation of incompetence, illness, anger and fatigue. Do you ever notice when you are sick and keep telling yourself and everyone around you that you are sick, the sicker you get?

"I Am" are two of the most powerful words in the English language. The bible teaches us about Moses at the burning bush. Moses asks, "When I go to the people, who shall I say sent me?" God replies, "Tell them, I Am has sent me to you." Earlier in their conversation, God stated, "I Am that I Am". When we use the words "I am" whatever follows is a declaration of who and/or what we believe about ourselves.

When you say to a child, "I am confident in your ability to make wise/healthy choices..." or "I am proud of and for you...you must be proud of yourself" or "I am so happy that you are my child", you are declaring a positive position and helping to build the child's (or individual's) self-confidence.

On the other hand, when you say to a child, "I am sick of you" or "I am sick and tired of your...." or "You make me sick" or "You make me angry", what you are declaring is the child is making you sick or angry. It is a very negative position to come from.

A child does not have the power to make a parent or person anything. Let me say that again, a child does not have the *power* to make a parent or person anything!

No one does, for that matter. Sick, mad, angry, frustrated and even happy are emotions that arise within us. They are emotions connected to adrenaline. It is a natural physiological response to an event, a circumstance or whatever. The emotion: angry, mad, sad, frustrated or happy is the label that we give to it. The adrenaline is the same with all emotions.

How we interpret the adrenaline rush, and how we react or respond to that feeling is OUR CHOICE. We don't choose the feeling...it just comes. Reacting is what we "act out" - many times, it is the mirrored reflection of how the child or other person is acting. If we act out against a child the way they act out at us, no one wins. Often when a child is throwing a temper tantrum, we throw one back.

We have the choice to respond by giving life to the situation or to react by adding fuel to the fire. You have a choice. You can take a deep breath and say to the child, "You have a right to your feelings and it is okay to <u>feel</u> angry, sad, upset or frustrated. What you do not have a right to do is act out by damaging anything, hitting your brother or sister, kicking the cat or dog, etc. There are consequences for disruptive or destructive behaviors and actions."

You can also begin by saying, "I love you <u>and</u> your words, actions or behaviors are inappropriate and there will be consequences." The key here is to use the word "and", not the word "but."

By using the word "and", you separate the child (person) from the actions and behaviors. I'll say that again, by using the word "and", you separate the child (person) from the behaviors. You teach the child (or person) that you love them <u>unconditionally</u>, even when you do not like or approve of their words, actions or behaviors.

Using the word "but" would void or cancel the, "I love you." It sounds as though you love the child (or person) conditionally.

It is very important to let the child know there is a consequence for inappropriate behavior. The child knows that if he/she acts out by hurting someone, destroying something or using foul language, there will be a consequence.

Keeping your word and following through with the consequence is also extremely important. It is the power of YOUR word. Be sure that the consequence does "fit the crime" – so to speak – don't go to the extremes for minor offenses, nor should there be minor consequences for major offenses.

If the consequence means the child is to be grounded for a week with no T.V. or computer games, then you may have to change your schedule to be home with the child – in order to enforce the consequences. Yes, it may be an inconvenience to you, but it is a necessity for positive change.

Nancy shared the following experience that she had with her own daughter, it demonstrates the powerful impact unconditional love and acceptance has on children.

When my daughter was in her "terrific twos" she began throwing temper tantrums. I learned that the most supportive and loving thing that I could do was to pick her up, take her to her room and sit her down in the middle of the floor.

I would say to her, "I love you and I understand that you are feeling unhappy. It is okay to feel angry, sad, frustrated, upset or what ever you are feeling. Mommy is going to sit right here in your room with you while you express what you are feeling."

I would then move away from her and sit on the floor next to the wall and watch. I would watch her from a feeling and expression of love – not anger or disgust.

If she started to throw a toy or be destructive, I would stop her and reinforce that she could kick, scream, cry, beat on a pillow, the bed or whatever she needed to do, as long as it did not hurt her, or me or damage anything.

Usually, within about 5 to 10 minutes of expressing her anger through crying, kicking, screaming, etc. she would calm down and crawl up in my lap to snuggle.

I would receive her with love and acceptance. Eventually she would sob herself to sleep. I know, that often during these times she was tired and fighting sleep. Additionally, I believe that she had a fear of abandonment – the number one fear of all human beings.

By my staying in the room with her, protecting her from injuring herself and allowing her to come to me for comfort, when she had exhausted her feelings, she felt reassured and secure enough to go to sleep.

When a situation like this arises, stop and think before you speak. Ask yourself, 'What will the impact of my words be?'

We, as parents and teachers, have the need to control children. For children to understand right choices from wrong choices, we need to give them options they can understand. With these options, children must also understand the consequences.

When we choose to discipline a child for unacceptable or inappropriate behavior and he/she doesn't understand why they are receiving discipline, they may never learn how to make good choices. And, they may never learn to accept the consequences associated with bad choices.

Responsibility

Taking responsibility for our words and actions is a powerful and assertive tool. Respond comes from the same root word as responsibility. To respond powerfully and from a place of love, we must choose our words carefully and consciously.

The power behind taking responsibility for our words usually diffuses the situation because people expect a defensive attitude.

When addressing a child with ADD, ADHD, Tourette syndrome or any other condition, we must speak confidence into their situations. The words we can use are, "You are a unique and exceptional child (person)", "You are a unique and divine creation", "You have the ability to make good choices" or "I am confident in your ability to make good/healthy decisions." "I am confident that when you make the right/healthy choice about ... you will follow through with it."

When a child does make inappropriate or unhealthy choices, in addition to experiencing the consequences of their choices, it is also essential to explore with them a very important question, *"How could you do this differently next time?"*

This is one of the most important times to truly listen and allow them to come up with some of their own alternatives. It is sometimes difficult for parents to keep our mouths shut and wait for their ideas to formulate.

IT IS ESSENTIAL that we give them time to think of alternatives. Once they have given us alternatives, then we can discuss the alternatives. This is a good time to praise them for the appropriate ideas – perhaps adding one or two of your own, with positive reinforcement, guidance and direction.

To forbid a child to do anything is almost impossible, especially when they get older. So, to instill in them at a young age that you are confident in their wisdom and ability to make good and healthy choices is affirming and supporting their self-confidence. Moving them in the direction of personal responsibility.

The power in these words gives them a sense of independence, and at the same time, helps to manifest good choices in their future.

"The power in the words you use will support and reinforce your child, while building confidence and self-esteem, so choose them carefully."

Nancy Harkins

Active Listening

Now that you understand how powerful your words can be, it is equally important to understand the power in active listening.

Over the years, my husband Bill has attended several conferences on listening. I asked him to share his experience and some guidelines on what I believe to be an important aspect in manifesting the power of words.

Bill's thoughts

Many people believe listening is a passive activity. Quite the contrary. The reason it is called active listening is because it requires a very active role on the part of the listener. In fact, to be a good active listener, you almost have to empty yourself of yourself, so you can focus properly on what the other person is saying. By providing this level of attention, you can really hear what they are actually saying - on all three levels.

I say three levels because we have three sets of ears. They are (1) our physical ears on our head, (2) the ears that exist in our mind and (3) the ears that exist in our heart.

Our physical ears hear the words, sounds, loudness or softness, pitch, etc. of what is being said. Our mental ears hear the emotion, urgency, tone and some interpretation of what is being said <u>and not said</u>. The ears of our heart hear the spiritual level and activity of what is being said <u>and not said</u>.

When you have all three sets of ears engaged in listening to someone, you are really very attentive to them, plus all of the things they are giving you to process.

People are very receptive to this. They will sense your level of attentiveness and know that you are really listening to them. This in itself will have a profound effect upon most people. The reason is – people are not used to being really listened to.

Ask yourself these questions:

- How many times has the person you are talking to finished your sentence for you or interrupted you while you were speaking?
- While talking to them were their eyes wandering all over the place?

If you have experienced this:

- Do you think they were really interested in what you were saying?
- Perhaps they were more interested in what their response was going to be to you?
- Perhaps their mind was on other thoughts or where they were going after they left you?

Before we get into an outline of the components and steps that will help you become a good active listener, I would like you to read several paragraphs from "Lessons in Lifemanship" by Bryan Bell.

"Active listening is particularly important in parental relationships with children. It comes as a surprise to many parents that they should have to listen to their children. They were brought up to believe that if you accept children as they are, they will remain that way, uncivilized and undeveloped, and that the best way to help them become something better in the future is to state what you don't accept about them now.

So, the treatment of most parents is heavy with evaluation, judgment, moralizing, preaching, admonishing, commanding and criticizing. But these are all actions and attitudes that cut off two-way communication between parents and children.

Parents wonder why their children will not talk to them, and they do not realize that the youngsters don't want to be preached to, disapproved of and put down.

Active listening is just as effective and important with teenagers and younger children as it is with adults, if not more so. This does not imply permissiveness, but does require love, a real desire to hear what the child has to say, a determination to be helpful, and a genuine ability to accept his or her feelings.

If these are present, and a parent can listen with appropriate verbal and nonverbal responses, proper feedback, and acceptance, while at the same time being non-judgmental, the results can be the same as in adult relationships. The child can be freed of troublesome feelings, and is less afraid of negative feelings in the future. A warmer, stronger relationship develops between parent and child.

Active listening also facilitates problem solving by the child. And, much to the amazement of the parents, the child is more willing to listen to parental thoughts and ideas. Shouldn't every parent want a child who is more self-directing, responsible and independent?"

If you would like to read more of "Lessons in Lifemanship" visit, www.bbll.com

Active listening can be applied to anyone you are listening to, not just to children. Keep in mind, active listening means more than just being willing to listen. It requires:

- **Intention** – capturing the intent of the child (or adult) speaking to you

- **Attention** – focus your whole being on what is being said to you

- **Participation** – become part of the interaction, not outside of it

By using the above active listening approach, you will save time, reduce errors, and create a climate of communication, cooperation and trust.

It is important to note: Active listening does not require the listener to agree with the other person, only to receive them where they are.

Steps to insure a climate for effective active listening include the following:

1. Seek to understand first and to be understood second.
2. Listen to, not against.
3. Evaluate, not value judge.
4. Watch for - what will not be said.
5. Read facial and body language.
6. Grasp feeling and content.
7. Restate - without repeating his/her words.

Examples of active listening for parents and teachers

The mother of the child throwing the temper tantrum is a perfect example of active listening. She grasped the *intention* of the child who was crying for help. Then, the mother gave her daughter *attention* rather than isolation. She accompanied her to her room, instead of sending her off alone to get over it. The mother *participated* by sitting down on the floor and allowing her child to cry until she was finished.

The daughter climbed up on her lap and fell asleep because of the climate created by the mother's actions – complete acceptance without condoning the actions, but without rejection.

The teacher who actively listened to Lene's son is another extraordinary example. Lene's son was disruptive in class because he always wanted to be the one to answer the teacher's questions.

His teacher captured the intent of the child and the class...what was being said by Lene's son and not being said by the class. She focused attention to the situation by finding a creative solution that included all concerned...the "Listening Chair". This taught Lene's son and others how to listen, while giving all of the children an opportunity to participate in answering questions.

Note: Active listening is an extensive subject and many books have been written on just listening alone. What I've tried to do in this area is provide an overview and outline for your reference and use. If this just wets your appetite, please obtain a more complete exploration of the subject through other sources.

Power of Words
Quick Guide

- **"I Am"** are the most powerful two words in the English language. What words follow, "I am" is a declaration of who and what we are.

- Power in words can manifest who and what we are. Think before you speak. Ask yourself, "How are my words going to affect the child/person?"

- Separate the behavior from the child/person. A child's/person's behavior has no power over you. How you respond is your responsibility and can <u>diffuse</u> a negative situation.

- Give a child/person choices and consequences. Follow through with consequences.

Speaking confidence and encouragement into a child's/person's life

- "You are a unique and exceptional child (individual)"
- "I trust you <u>will</u> make a good decision (or choice)"
- "I am confident in your ability to make good/healthy decisions…when you decide to…"

Active listening requires

- Intention – capturing the intent of the person speaking.
- Attention – focus on what is being said to you.
- Participation – become part of interaction, not outside of it.

chapter 7

Healthy Food Program

Now that you have been exposed to the importance of the first two parts of the Triumph Over Paradigm: Open Thinking and the Power of Words, the next step is to introduce you to the "Healthy Food Program".

The paradigm is most effective when incorporating all three parts, however, even if you do not utilize the first two parts, **using the "Healthy Food Program" alone can bring about positive results.**

As you have learned, there is a connection between certain foods, food additives, mood and behavior. When these foods and food additives are eliminated, or consumed in very limited quantities, a noticeable improvement is evident within a very short period of time. The four real life stories of triumph in Part One are testimonies to this fact.

To help you successfully transition into a healthy food program, the tools listed below are provided in the pages that follow:

- Weekly planner
- Suggested meals
- Guide to getting started
- Shopping list
- Lidle Café cookbook

Before guiding you through the process of preparing a plan, it is important to reflect on your own eating habits. Ask yourself these questions:

- Are you setting a healthy example for your family?
- What are you eating first thing in the morning and last thing at night?
- What snacks are you nibbling on throughout the day?
- Are you eating the very foods that may be affecting your own mental and physical health or that of your family?

Looking back at my own childhood, I can clearly see why my mother allowed us to have so much sugar and fast food. She worked very long hours to provide for us and by the end of the day, she was too exhausted to prepare dinner. On the weekends, she made up for it by baking pastries. Baking was an emotional release for my mother. Eating freshly baked pastries comforted all three of us. At the time, my mother didn't how much the sugars and the chemicals in food were affecting my attention span and Tourette syndrome.

Given the time constraints and pressures of daily life today, parents may have to reexamine their priorities for the sake of their families and themselves. Are you ready to reexamine your priorities? If you are, then begin by giving some thought to the following questions:

Is your diet revolving around:

- Pacifying your children?
- Your need for a moment of peace?
- Your work schedule?
- Activities your children are involved in at school?
- Stress or a combination of these and other factors?

Preparing A Weekly Plan

When you make the choice to give a healthy food program a try, begin by preparing a weekly plan for yourself first. It will be much easier to gain the confidence of your children and family when you have experienced personal success with the program.

Partnering

Partnering is when two people agree to do something together and become each other's support. In this case, eat the same foods and drink the same beverages.

If you have trouble motivating yourself, partner with your child, spouse or a good friend. One of the reasons I was successful in changing my diet, when I was first diagnosed with breast cancer, was the support of my husband, Bill. He ate the same things I did and continues to do so today.

Before preparing your weekly plan, make a list of foods and beverages you are buying on a regular basis. Check the labels for caffeine, MSG, and food colorings (see pages 89,94,95). Then read the effects of these ingredients by looking them up in the "Consumer's Dictionary of Food Additives." Choose which items you are going to eliminate from your diet.

I highly recommend taking a copy of, "A Consumer's Dictionary Guide of Food Additives" with you to the store. Also, familiarize yourself with the sections in this book including: foods to avoid, additives, hidden sources of MSG, brainy breakfasts, smart lunches, clever dinners, savvy snacks, brain boosting foods and the shopping list.

In order for you to succeed on a healthy food program, you must be prepared. Have plenty of healthy foods in your kitchen, at all times. If you don't, it is much too easy to go out for fast food or fall back to your old standbys.

Once you have empowered yourself with knowledge and some experience, it is time to put your healthy food program into action.

Start by choosing a few simple recipes from the Lidle Café cookbook to prepare. Try some new cereal; use rice or quinoa pasta next time you prepare spaghetti; try corn chips, instead of potato chips; try a brain smoothie; spread almond butter on a piece of whole grain bread instead of peanut butter; use almonnaise instead of mayonnaise the next time you make a tuna fish sandwich; bake a turkey breast instead of buying luncheon meat; make popcorn the old fashioned way over the stove top with olive oil and sea salt, etc.

After you have done your healthy food program for a while and feel comfortable and confident with it, pick a time to present it to your child or family. Present foods to them you think they will like or some of the information in this book you think they will agree with. Then, partner up and celebrate the new adventure!

Some ideas of how you can present a healthy food program to your child

Address the issue in a loving and non-threatening manner. Let the child know you love them "unconditionally" (with or without their disorder or syndrome).

Say, "I love you and you are a unique and special child (or person). As you know Dr. so and so, says you have ADD (or whatever condition) and recommends you be put on medication. How do you feel about that?"

Wait for the child's answer and then discuss their feelings. Offer an alternative approach including: eliminating certain foods and adding others to their diet, before conceding to medication. Ask the child how he or she feels about a change in diet?

The following scenarios will help you to approach the subject of eating healthy foods:

• (you speaking) - "There are healthy foods that taste really good. They will help you to concentrate and settle down. Mommy (or I) will eat these foods too. I will eat the same things you do, so we can both feel better. What do you think? Do you want to give it a try?"

• *How Stephanie presented a healthy food program to her nine-year old son, Stephen.* "Stephen, you know I am with you all the way on this. I am not going to abandon you. There are certain foods we are going to stop buying, just for a while, to see if they were adding to your problems. Some of the new foods are good for the brain. Would you like to try some of them? I will try them with you and together we can decide which ones we like.

Together, we will make a plan. Beginning on Monday through Friday, let's try not eating anything with sugar or caffeine in it. This means no soda. Is that okay with you? Then Friday after school we can pick two things we can cheat on. Saturday too! On Sunday night we will start all over again. Will you try this with me?"

• If the child is older, consider this approach: "I just learned the most interesting things about food ingredients. They may be affecting your ability to focus and concentrate. Wouldn't it be great if by changing some of the foods we eat you could feel better? I'm going shopping tomorrow and I will pick up a few new things to try. Do you want to come with me?

Would you like to read some of the information I discovered? Have you ever looked at the ingredients listed on the label before you opened the package? Do you want to learn what the words mean? Did you know food coloring could be affecting you and me in a negative way? Let's just see if there's something to this. I'll do it too.

Monday through Friday let's try some new foods and let's work on eliminating sugar and caffeine on these days. What do you say, are you in?"

• "Wouldn't it be great if some different foods would help your attention span and help you to focus better? If they do, maybe we can work with the doctor on getting you off the medication. Let's both try these foods together."

• "Wow, I just learned some really interesting information about some things that may be making your condition worse. I would really appreciate it if you read the information and gave me your feedback. I would like to know what you think. There may be something to it, especially for you. When you choose to try some new foods, I am confident you will do great."

5 *Steps*
To Making A Weekly Plan

1. Follow the example on the next page.
2. Make your weekly plan on an 8 ½ x 11 sheet of paper or if you are making a weekly plan with a young young child, use a poster board. Use stickers, stars and pictures of vegetables and fruits to make the plan look more fun.
3. Take at least one hour each week to make the weekly plan and allow yourself time to do the shopping.
4. Be realistic. Don't try to give up everything all at once.
5. Put your weekly plan on the refrigerator door.

Helpful Tips:

• Celebrate your new healthy food program by having a party. Make it fun.

• Begin each day with 8-12 oz water. Buy extra water, if you don't have filtered water. You will need to drink more water when cutting down on or eliminating the beverages you have been used to.

• Buy plenty of healthy snack foods like: blue corn chips, almond butter, fruit sweetened jam or fruit spread, whole grain crackers and the least processed cheese you can find. Chop up carrots, celery, zucchini etc. and have healthy salad dressing in the fridge to dip veggies in.

Sample of a Weekly Plan

WEEK ONE

	MON	TUE	WED	THUR	FRI	SAT	SUN
BREAKFAST							
SNACK							
LUNCH							
SNACK							
DINNER							

• Foods I am giving up this week:
• Foods and beverages I am cutting down on:

Closer Look at a Weekly Plan

WEEK ONE

	MONDAY	TUESDAY
Upon Rising	glass of water	glass of water
BREAKFAST	cereal, flaxseeds, banana, raspberries and orange juice	toast, almond butter, with flaxseed and a smart smoothie
SNACK	apple	no snack today
LUNCH	veggie sandwich, blue corn chips, fruit popsicle	Rainbow salad in a pita pocket, few pieces of cheese
SNACK	energy candy	celery, carrot sticks with hummus dip
DINNER	Rainbow salad with baked turkey breast and potatoes no dessert today.	Fish, brown rice salad, no-bake apple pie

- Foods I am giving up this week: Doughnuts, French Fries
- Foods and beverages I am cutting down on: Soda – One can every other day, Monday-Friday no more ice cream before bedtime

Brainy Breakfasts, Smart Lunches, Clever Dinners, Savvy Snacks

As I've stated before, parents are observing that there is a relationship between what children eat and drink and how they think, act and learn. The brain uses 20-25 percent of the total energy a person consumes. It makes sense to feed the brain healthy foods so it can work better.

The following examples: brainy breakfasts, smart lunches, clever dinners and savvy snacks are a good place to begin feeding the brain the food it needs to work properly.

How children begin the day sets the mood for the rest of the day. "Children who eat a breakfast containing both complex carbohydrates and proteins tend to show better learning and performance than children who eat primarily a high protein or high carbohydrate breakfast. Breakfasts high in carbohydrates with little protein seem to sedate children rather than stimulate their brain to learn" source: www.askdrsears.com

• Recipes for Brainy Breakfast, Smart Lunches and Clever Dinners are found in the Lidle Café cookbook.

10 Brainy Breakfasts

1. Whole grain cereal with sliced banana, strawberries, and raspberries, sprinkled with ground flaxseeds and a few almonds or walnuts. Rice, Almond or Organic Soy Milk.

2. Oatmeal with honey, cinnamon, sliced apples and raisins with ground flaxseeds sprinkled on top. A glass of orange juice.

3. Whole grain or sprouted toast with almond butter, ground flaxseeds and sliced bananas on top. Add a little honey. A few slices of apple. Orange or apple juice or organic soymilk.

4. A glass of juiced vegetables. Whole grain toast with almond butter, jam and ground flaxseeds.

5. Granola covered with yogurt (preferably without hormones in it and without fruit on bottom) sliced bananas or berries. Orange or apple juice or a glass of freshly juiced apples alone or apples/carrots juice.

6. Any one of the Smart Smoothies.

7. Veggie omelet, scrambled eggs or scrambled tofu eggs. Orange or apple juice

8. Rice waffles, maple syrup, ground flaxseeds, sliced fruit on top (strawberries, bananas, raspberries, blueberries). A few almonds, pecans or walnuts. A glass of organic soymilk or almond milk.

9. Whole grain pancakes, maple syrup, berries, ground flaxseed, yogurt and a glass of apple juice.

10. Whole grain muffin and "Brain Smoothie".

10 Smart Lunches

1. Rainbow salad, blue corn chips & hummus dip and an apple.

2. Veggie sandwich on whole grain bread, yellow corn chips and an apple.

3. Vegetarian chili, blue corn chips, carrot and celery sticks, energy candy.

4. Almond butter & jam sandwich and a few slices of apple.

5. Smart smoothie and a few celery sticks with almond butter.

6. Turkey or tuna fish sandwich with almonnaise, lettuce & tomato, rainbow salad and your choice of energy candy, orange-date bars or an apple.

7. Garden salad wrap with a glass of fresh vegetable juice (can put grilled or baked chicken in wrap).

8. Grilled vegetable wrap (optional: turkey or free range chicken slices).

9. Pita sandwich filled with lettuce, cucumber, avocado, tomato, almonnaise and/or hummus (or fill pita with rainbow salad), blue corn chips.

10. Bowl of fruit with almonds and walnuts or just a brain smoothie (great as a breakfast replacement).

10 Clever Dinners

1. Vegetable pasta primavera with brown rice pasta and rainbow salad.

2. Baked turkey breast with potato casserole surprise, rainbow salad (or salad of your choice).

3. Salmon nuggets, steamed broccoli and French vegetable soup. Applesauce for dessert.

4. Tuna fish with almonnaise on sprouted bread, blue corn chips and sliced carrot, celery and zucchini sticks with hummus and salsa dip.

5. Vegetarian chili and blue corn chips. Frozen fruit popsicles or frozen fruit gelato from champion juicer for dessert.

6. French vegetable soup, rainbow salad and no-bake apple pie for dessert.

7. Pistachio pasta with corn quinoa elbow macaroni and salad. Rice dream ice cream bar for dessert.

8. Rainbow salad (or a salad of your choice) with crackers and cheese and orange-date dessert bars.

9. Grilled turkey burger or baked garden burger with salad and grilled zucchini.

*10.*Sauteed vegetable wrap with chicken or turkey. Blue corn chips, salsa and guacamole dip.

14 Savvy Snacks

1. **Nuts & seeds** –raw and unsalted
Almonds, pecans, walnuts, sunflower and pumpkin.

2. **Celery & almond butter logs**
Cut celery stick in quarters and spread almond butter in the middle of the celery. Put a few raisins or dried cranberries on top and call them, "black ant logs or fire ant logs" for young kids.

3. **Energy candy**

4. **Almond butter & jam sandwich**
Toasted or un-toasted sprouted bread with almond butter and jam or fruit spread.

5. **Blue corn chips with hummus or guacamole dip**

6. **Odwalla Bar, energy or protein bar** (read labels!)
Tastes great! Just like dessert. If you can't get, it ask your grocery store to order it in for you. Cranberry "C" Monster is my favorite.

7. **Carob chips, carob coated raisins or nuts**

8. **Fruit popsicles** (without any food coloring)

9. **Whole grain cracker with a piece of cheese**

10. **Smart smoothies**

11. **Raisins (**try carob coated raisins and trail mix)

12. **Bowl of cereal** or a handful of dry cereal

13. **Fresh fruit or dried fruit** (unsulfured)

14. **Applesauce** unsweetened (mix in ground flaxseed)

Brain Boosting Foods

- **Flaxseed** - rich source of omega 3 fatty acid. Omega 3 fatty acids are necessary for proper infant growth and development. They are especially important in the formation of a healthy nervous system and help keep that nervous system functioning properly. Rich source of protein.

- **Nuts** – raw and unsalted, especially Brazil and walnuts contain high amounts of choline, which is a precursor to acetylcholine (a neurochemcial that plays an important role in cognition and reasoning.)

- **Sunflower and pumpkin seeds** – raw and unsalted, contain zinc, which not only boosts the immune system, it improves brain function.

- **Berries** - (dark colored) contain a substance called proanthrocyanidins, which are powerful antioxidants that cross the blood brain barrier and protect the brain from deteriorating.

- **Black and yellow beans** - contain high amounts of tryptophan, which has a calming effect on the nerves.

- **Lettuce and celery** - foods for calming and un-stressing (try green leafy lettuce instead of iceberg lettuce).

- **Fish**- deep-water fish including tuna, flounder, sardines and salmon. High in choline - a memory booster.

- **Dark green leafy vegetables and citrus fruits** - contain folic acid and protect the brain and memory: spinach, kale, broccoli and all green vegetables.

• **Water** – is the "King of Beverages" for the brain!

The human body is composed of about 70% water. The body's water supply is responsible for and involved in nearly every bodily process, including digestion, absorption, circulation, and excretion. Water is also the primary transporter of nutrients throughout the body and is necessary for all building functions in the body. Water helps maintain normal body temperature and is essential for carrying waste material out of the body.

Replacing the water that is continually being lost through sweating and elimination is very important. It is essential to drink at least <u>eight 8-ounce glasses</u> of quality water each day.

Though caffeinated beverages contain water, they cause the body to excrete more water than it actually takes in. The result is less fluid then you had to begin with. The majority of Americans are chronically dehydrated. Mild dehydration can slow down one's metabolism as much as 5%. A University of Washington study showed one glass of water shut down hunger pangs for almost 100% of the dieters studied.

Lack of water is the number one trigger of daytime fatigue. **A mere 2% drop in body water can trigger fuzzy short-term memory, trouble with basic math and difficulty focusing on the computer screen or on a printed page.**

How much water to drink:

• ½ ounce of water for every pound of body weight. If you are very active, then 2 to 3 times the above for every pound of body weight. For example: if you weigh 120lbs., you need to drink 60 ounces of water each day.

Brain Boosters

- Apples
- Avocados
- Beets
- Black Strap Molasses
- Blueberries
- Broccoli, Brussels Sprouts
- Brown Rice
- Curry
- Cauliflower, Celery
- Cereal – whole grain
- Cantaloupe, Cherries
- Celtic Sea Salt
- Chicken – free range
- Eggs
- Fruit All Are Great!
- Flaxseeds, Flaxseed Oil
- Grapes
- Granola, Honey
- Milk -Rice, Almond, Soy
- Nuts – almonds, walnuts, pecans, organic soy nuts
- Almond, Cashew Butter
- Extra Virgin Olive Oil
- Oatmeal –not instant
- Peas, Purple Cabbage
- Potatoes
- Radishes
- Raspberries, Strawberries
- Salmon
- Spinach
- Turkey
- Vegetables All Are Great!
- Yogurt - without fruit

Brain Bombers

- Artificial Food Colorings
- Artificial Ingredients
- Artificial Sweeteners
- Caffeine
- Soda
- Energy Drinks with added Caffeine, Panax Ginseng, Ma Huang or Guarana
- Candy with food colorings or artificial sweeteners
- Corn Syrup
- Hydrogenated Oils
- Instant Sauces
- Instant Puddings, Gelatin
- MSG – Excitotoxins
- Packaged Lunch Meats
- Margarine, Spreads
- Micro Wave Popcorn with Artificial Butter
- Processed Cheese
- Soda & Diet Soda
- White Flour Foods, White Bread
- Marijuana & Other Drugs

PART THREE

Getting Started

Chapter 8

Getting Started

"It takes 21 days to make a habit
and 30 days to make a lifestyle change"

In this chapter, you are provided with a specific guide to help you get started. First, choose the level you want to start at from the choices below. Then, from each of the three parts of the Triumph Over Paradigm make one or more selections.

Beginners Level – "Ease" your way into getting started

Pick only one or two choices from each part of the paradigm – Adopt Open Thinking, Power of Words and Healthy Food Program –pages 150, 151, 152 and 153.

Your goal is to make <u>realistic</u> choices from each one of the parts and stick to it for 30 days. Once you have mastered your initial choices, continue on by making one or two new choices for the next 30 days...and so on...and so on. After two or three months, you will be ready for the intermediate level.

Feel free to make additional choices if you are breezing through the beginners level within a few weeks. Choose these from any one part or all parts of the paradigm.

147

Intermediate Level – 5 days on, 2 days off

For those of you who want to see noticeable improvement within 30 days. Pick two choices from each of the first two parts of the paradigm – Adopt Open Thinking and Power of Words.

From <u>Monday–Friday</u>, follow the healthy food program outlined in this book. This means avoiding all foods with additives including all of the ones listed on pages 93,94 and 95. On <u>Saturday and Sunday</u>, choose two cheat foods and one cheat beverage each day.

This does not mean that on Saturday you buy one gallon of ice cream and eat the whole thing and call it your one cheat food. Or, buying a six pack of cola and calling it your cheat beverage. It means, one can of cola and one ice cream bar! Come Monday morning, the 5 days <u>on </u>begins again. Use the shopping list as a guide (page 156).

Advanced Level – "Kick Butt"

Take a few weeks to one month to prepare for the advanced level. Pick two chooses from each of the first two parts of the paradigm while preparing for the 30 days of "Kick Butt" healthy eating.

The advanced program means reading all the labels on every item of food or beverage brought into your home. It may also mean not going out to eat for 30 days or being very careful of what is ordered. All of the information you need to help you with ingredients and additives is included in this book. Sometimes it's difficult to monitor what a child eats away from home, so just do the best you can. You will do great!

Eat and drink everything you currently have at home or give it away. Stock your cupboards and refrigerator with the items listed on the Shopping List, page156. Practice preparing recipes from the Lidle Café cookbook, especially the five favorite recipes listed on page 154. Make plenty of soup and vegetarian chili to freeze. They will come in handy.

Choosing the advanced level will mean a little more work for you, but the rewards are great. Rearrange your schedule if you have to. If you are partnering with your child, explain the "Kick Butt" program and make it sound fun! Make it a challenge.

It may be necessary to make your child's lunch for school everyday. You may have to send a note to his teachers or to the school, alerting them to the food program your child is on.

If you know ahead of time when the teacher is bringing in sweets, make sure to pack a healthy sweet for your child, so he or she will not feel deprived.

There may be some withdrawal symptoms if you do not ease yourself, children or family into the advanced program. Symptoms may include: feeling tired for the first few days, headachy and irritable. These are withdrawal side effects of caffeine, sugar and harmful food additives! Symptoms can be mild if a person consumes lots of water and nibbles often throughout the day.

How to Adopt Open Thinking

**Pick 1 or 2 or more choices
and commit to following through for 30 days**

- Read the book, "Excitotoxins, The Taste That Kills" by Dr. Russell L. Blaylock.

- Read the book, "Talking Back To Ritalin", by Dr. Peter R. Breggin.

- Purchase the book, "A Consumer's Dictionary Of Food Additives", by Ruth Winter, M.S. and take it with you each time you go grocery shopping.

- Purchase a copy of the Physicians Desk Reference (PDR) or reference a copy at the library or go to the Internet at www.PDR.net - check out the warnings and side-effects of the drug or drugs you or your child are taking (or are recommended to take).

- If you or your child has been diagnosed, get a second opinion (naturopathic medical doctor, naturopathic doctor or qualified herbalist).

- Read up on non-drug approaches.

- Attend seminars and classes.

- Attend a support group and/or parent group.

- Take a course on natural health.

How to Manifest the Power of Words

**Pick 1 or 2 or more choices
and commit to following through for 30 days**

Speaking to yourself – every day

- "I am confident, I can commit to my healthy choices for 30 days"
- "I am a good parent"
- "I can commit to preparing a weekly plan"
- "I am capable of making good decisions"

Speaking to a child and/or adult – once a day

- "I am happy/proud you are my son, daughter, husband"
- "I am confident in your ability to make good choices"
- "I love you and your behavior is unacceptable"
- "You are capable of anything you set your mind to"
- "You are a unique and exceptional child (or person)"
- "I am confident, you have the ability to complete a task"
- "Yes you have symptoms of (ADD, ADHD or Tourette syndrome) and you are smart, capable, unique, creative and loving"

Active Listening

- Really listen to your child, spouse, partner for 10 minutes every day
- Practice Intention, Attention and Participation (pg.123)

How to Begin a Healthy Food Program

**Pick 1 or 2 or more choices
and commit to following through for 30 days**

Foods I am cutting down on or eliminating

- Soda (diet and regular)
  I will dilute soda with 50% water
- Any food with MSG on the label or at least one or two
  foods I am currently buying which contain MSG
- Any food with excitotoxins in it or at least one or
  two foods I am currently buying with excitotoxins
- Artificial sweeteners
- Fast food from fast food restaurants
- Buttered or flavored microwave popcorn
- Red meat
- Flavored potato chips
- Energy drinks with added caffeine
- Canned or instant soups (check label)
- Instant breakfast, lunch or dinner foods
- Instant puddings and/or gelatin
- Candy with MSG or excitotoxins
- Yogurt with fruit on bottom (check label)
- Flavored crackers
- Luncheon meat and artificial meat
- Processed cheese individually wrapped with plastic
- Cheese spreads
- Steak sauces
- White table salt
- White bread
- Coffee with caffeine

Healthy foods I am adding to my weekly plan

- Water
- Olive oil
- Fresh fruits every day (at least one)
- Fresh vegetables every day (at least celery or carrot sticks on days with no salad)
- Celtic sea salt
- Nuts – raw almonds, pecans, walnuts, cashews
- Rice milk, almond milk and/or organic soymilk
- Free range chicken – hormone free
- Turkey – hormone free
- Fish –salmon, tuna
- Almonnaise
- Least processed cheese (any cheese that doesn't bend or feel like rubber)
- Whole grain and/or sprouted breads
- Smart smoothies
- Real fruit popsicles
- Protein bars (check label)
- Dried un-sulfured fruit without added sugar
- Raisins
- Applesauce, unsweetened
- Real fruit juices, not from concentrate
- Rice pasta, corn quinoa pasta, soy pasta
- Almond butter
- Fruit sweetened jams and fruit spreads
- Rice waffles
- Whole grain pancake mix
- Real honey, instead of sugar
- Organic chocolate
- Caffeine free herbal teas
- Ground flaxseeds and/or flaxseed oil

5 Favorite recipes to get started

These five recipes are winners. They are a strong foundation to build upon. The recipes appear in the Lidle Café Cookbook.

• **Almonnaise** - A fabulous substitute for mayonnaise. Your children and family will love it. Almonnaise is good with tuna fish, turkey or chicken sandwiches, veggie sandwiches, potato salad and macaroni (corn quinoa) salad. Even those who don't like mayonnaise, like almonnaise!

• **Vegetable Pasta Primavera** - Simple, simple, simple to make. This is a recipe your kids will want to help make after they've done it once. They can create their own version of Primavera.

• **Rainbow Salad** - Lasts in refrigerator for three to four days and gets better with each passing day. Add lettuce, as you need it. Rainbow Salad is great without lettuce, with soy pasta added to it, in a pita pocket or rolled in a tortilla with lettuce to make a veggie wrap.

• **Vegetarian Chili** — Everyone's favorite. The perfect food to freeze and have on hand for anytime.

• **No Bake Apple Pie** - Your family won't ever know it hasn't been baked.

Tips for success

- Have at least one or two items in your freezer, for when you don't have time to prepare anything. Start with French vegetable soup and vegetarian chili.
- Always have healthy marinara sauce and a variety of rice, corn quinoa and soy pastas in the cupboard.
- Always have frozen fruit available for smart smoothies.
- Have extra almond, soy and rice milk in the cupboard.
- Make a batch of rainbow salad every week for 30 days.

Tips for eating out

- Avoid buffets, unless it is a salad bar that boasts on using only fresh ingredients. If you have to go to a buffet, other than a salad bar buffet, always have your child or children begin with salad and/or soup. Allow them to choose only one dessert and stop at one serving. Avoid all processed meats. Teach them to take small portions and after finishing their plate, they can go back for more.

- When eating at a Chinese, Japanese or Thai restaurant, ask them not to add any MSG to your order. A few years ago I wanted to eat at a Chinese restaurant. The hostess insisted they did not use MSG. I told her I would go into shock if I had MSG. She whispered, "Yes, we use MSG."

- Right after the water is brought to the table, have your children drink a glass while waiting for their order. Make a contest out of it, see who can finish theirs first.

- Avoid fried foods and order baked or broiled foods instead.

155

Shopping List

The following list will help you get started making the transition into the healthy food program. If your local grocery or health food store does not stock these items, ask them to order them for you.

If they won't, then you may be able to get these items in quantity from Mountain Peoples Distributing. There is a minimum dollar requirement. Ask a few of your friends to choose the foods they want and make a collective co-op order. I believe they can deliver to most states. Their phone number is listed on the resource page 220.

Please, do not let this shopping list intimidate you! These are most of the things I keep stocked in my own kitchen. Keep in mind that I have been living a healthy lifestyle for five years now. This list is a comprehensive list of foods that have taken me years to discover.

Start slowly by choosing a few items to try first. Remember, Rome wasn't built in one day. This list is only a guide to help you along. You may discover foods you enjoy that are not on this list. Be adventuresome and discover new and flavorful healthy foods.

• SPICES
Name Brand: The Spice Hunter and Frontier are good (or your favorite brand)
- Italian Seasoning
- Fajita Seasoning
- Coriander
- Pesto Seasoning
- Cumin
- Oregano Flakes, Basil Leaf

Name Brand: A. Vogel
- Herbamare - organic herb seasoning salt (my favorite spice)

- Celtic Sea Salt – has important minerals left in the salt
- Hungarian Hot Paprika
- Organic Vegetarian Worcestershire Sauce (no Excitotoxins)
- Vegetable Bouillon (Rapunzel brand) no MSG,
  www.rapunzel.com

• ALMOND BUTTER
(raw or toasted almond butter)

• JAM or JELLY or FRUIT SPREAD
(fruit sweetened)

• PASTA
- Name Brand - Lunderg and Ancient Quinoa Harvest
 (There are other name brands that are also good)
- Organic Soy Pasta
- Brown Rice Pasta
- Spelt Pasta
- Lentil Pasta
- Quinoa Pasta *(pronounced Keen-wa)*

• FROZEN FOODS
- Name Brand: Amy's is good. There are lots of good frozen
  pre-packaged foods on the market (read labels)
- Pizza, Enchiladas & more

• BREAD
(Look for sprouted breads or whole grain breads. They
are healthier and easier to digest)
- Ezekiel Bread
- Spelt and Sprouted Grain Breads
- Pita Bread

- **BEANS & RICE**
  - Black, navy, pinto, lentil
  - Brown Rice

- **FROZEN WAFFLES**
  - Name Brand: Van's Wheat Free and Rice Waffles
  (there are other good brands. Look for gluten free
  and wheat free)

- **FRESH VEGETABLES**
  It's easier for you to eat healthy if you have as many of these
  veggies in your refrigerator at all times.
  - Carrots, celery, cucumber, corn
  - Broccoli
  - Potatoes
  - Garlic
  - Tomatoes
  - Red, Green & Yellow Bell Pepper
  - Lettuce- Romaine, red leaf, green leaf
  - Spinach, kale
  - Eggplant
  - Zucchini
  - Broccoli
  - Cauliflower
  - Long Green Beans
  - Onions & Shallots
  - Parsley

- **FRESH FRUIT**
  - Bananas, all kinds of berries, apples, peaches, pears.

- **FROZEN FRUIT**
  (Great in cereal and smart smoothies)
  - Blueberries, Raspberries, Mango, Strawberries

- **SALAD DRESSINGS**
  Name Brand: Annie's Dressings are really good
  - Tuscany
  - Caesar
  - Raspberry

- **APPLESAUCE** unsweetened

- **NUTS & SEEDS**
  - Raw Almonds
  - Cashews
  - Walnuts
  - Pumpkin Seeds
  - Sesame Seeds
  - Sunflower Seeds
  Soaking nuts and seeds in water for 8 hours before
  eating starts the enzyme action and they are easier to
  chew and digest. After soaking, pat dry with a paper
  towel and always refrigerate afterwards...only
  lasts three days.

- **BOXED CEREAL**
  - Health Valley Organic Fiber 7-Multigrain Flakes
  - Arrowhead Mills Organic Amaranth Flakes
  - Erewhon Crispy Brown Rice (just like Rice Krispies)
  - Granola

- **FLAXSEED** and/or flaxseed oil
  Grind seeds and put in cereal, on toast, juice or a green
  nutrition drink.

- **VEGANAISE** (mayonnaise substitute or make the
  almonnaise in the Lidle Café cookbook).

- **ORGANIC TOFU**
  (for scrambled tofu eggs)

- **SALSA** (if you can't get or make it fresh, it's best to buy brands with short expiration dates, not those that last for a year or more)

- **HUMMUS DIP**
  (garbanzo beans, garlic, lemon, tahini)

- **EXTRA VIRGIN OLIVE OIL**

- **BLUE CORN or YELLOW CORN TORTILLA CHIPS** (preferably with sea salt)

- **FREE RANGE CHICKEN**
  (free range, no hormones)

- **TURKEY**
  (free range, no hormones)

- **FISH**
  - Salmon or a deep-water fish, tuna fish

- **FROZEN FRUIT POPSCIKLES** (no food coloring, look for ones with real fruit not just fruit concentrate)

- **RICE DREAM ICE CREAM**

Lidle Café

cookbook

How the Lidle Café came to be...

Named after Bill & Agi Lidle
this festive café for two
serves divinely inspired dishes
while enjoying a pines view
our hats off to chef Agi
whose past attempts were "Peeu"
either burnt or too soggy
menu selection was few
her efforts never wavered
as she prayed for the passion to cook
the prayers were soon answered
delicious recipes now appear in this book

Get your kids involved in helping to prepare some of these recipes. It's a wonderful time to spend with your child. There are products on the market that make interactive cooking with your kid's fun. Products like the "spiral dicer" make zucchini, cucumber, sweet potato and squash look like angel hair pasta. Kids love to play with their food and they'll love angel hair vegetables. Most of the Lidle Café favorites are festive and colorful.

You may be saying to yourself, "I hate to cook" or "I don't have time to cook" or "What if I fail and the recipe doesn't turn out?"

Five years ago, when I first embarked on a healthy food program I was LOST! The kitchen was where I spent the least amount of my time. In the beginning (and sometimes even today) I ruined lots of recipes. Some were awful! It's a good thing I had a well-stocked kitchen, so there was always backup. For a while, cereal and almond butter sandwiches saved the day!

As time went on, I got better and better and better. Today I give cooking classes and everyone comments that I'm a chef. It's fun because I feel like a chef when I'm in the kitchen. I've learned how to combine different spices to make the same dish taste completely different. It has taken time but it has been well worth it.

Please don't feel nervous or intimidated. Give some of my recipes a try. Begin with some of the easiest recipes first. You and your family will be better for it.

A champion juicer is a great investment. Not only can you juice fresh vegetables, you can make frozen fruit ice cream in minutes. Just freeze some fruit, including bananas, and run it through the juicer! Everyone loves fresh frozen fruit ice cream.

Have Fun!

Soup Du Jour

Creamy Corn Chowder

Refreshing Carrot Soup

Vegetarian Chili

French Vegetable Soup

Flu and Cold Season Vegetable Broth

Creamy Corn Chowder

When fresh corn is in season, this soup is delicious. Watch kids eat it up!

- ➢ 4 cups fresh corn kernels (about 4 ears of corn)
- ➢ 1 teaspoon ground cumin
- ➢ 2 cups almond milk
- ➢ 2 teaspoons of minced onion
- ➢ Big pinch of Celtic sea salt
- ➢ Big pinch Herbamare Seasoning
- ➢ Few shakes of garlic powder
- ➢ 1 teaspoon flaxseed oil
- ➢ 1 avocado in small chunks

In a blender, combine most of the corn, almond milk, most of the avocado, cumin, and seasonings. Blend well and then stir in (not blend in) remaining corn. If it's too thick add a little more almond milk. Decorate with a little corn on top with a few avocado chunks.

Lidle Café Twists: Substitute shallots for onions, sprinkle small pieces of red pepper on top with a sprinkle of Hungarian Paprika for garnish. Try it first the way the recipe reads, if it's not to your taste add your own twists like jalapeno, sweet basil, even a little curry. Serves 3-4

Refreshing Carrot Soup

- ➢ 1 cup fresh carrot juice (use a juicer or vita mix)
- ➢ 1/2 -1 avocado
- ➢ 1 teaspoon or more lemon juice
- ➢ 1 clove or more garlic
- ➢ Big pinch Celtic sea salt
- ➢ Big pinch ground cumin
- ➢ Big pinch coriander

In a blender, combine carrot juice and avocado. Add cumin, coriander, lemon juice, salt and garlic. Save a few pieces of avocado to garnish the top of the soup.

Lidle Café Twists: Try adding grated ginger, jalapeno, chopped red and green peppers, thinly sliced celery, sweet basil, corn kernels, bite size chunks of zucchini...even a little curry powder.

I find with carrot soup, most people like a small serving with salad or main course.

Recipe serves 1-2

Vegetarian Chili

Everyone loves fresh chili. They ask for the recipe all the time, but I've never measured any of the ingredients before, so here it goes. Remember you can always add more or less...to your liking. This chili freezes well. It's always good for a back up.

- ➢ 1 cup pinto beans
- ➢ 1 cup navy beans
- ➢ 1 cup black beans
- ➢ 3 carrots sliced thin
- ➢ 2 white or yellow onions minced
- ➢ 3 green peppers diced
- ➢ 4-5 stalks celery chopped medium
- ➢ 3 zucchini sliced medium
- ➢ 4-6 tablespoons chili powder
- ➢ 3-4 teaspoons Celtic sea salt
- ➢ At least 4 cloves of garlic minced (if you love garlic, leave some extra whole pieces in)
- ➢ 4 or more tablespoons Cumin
- ➢ 4 tablespoons of Turmeric
- ➢ 2 16oz cans of peeled tomatoes or 5-7 fresh tomatoes peeled (blanch in boiling water for a minute before peeling)
- ➢ 1 - 16oz can of tomato puree

Put beans in a bowl and cover with water. Soak overnight. The next day, rinse the beans with water and put them in the big pot you're cooking the chili in. Fill with water (about four inches above beans).

Bring to a boil and lower heat to slow cook for one hour (after 30 minutes, check to see if the water level is okay. If it's cooked down too close to the beans, add a little more.)

When beans are cooked, after one hour there should be 2-3 inches of water over the beans. While the beans are boiling, skim off the brown residue on top.

A few minutes before the beans have finished cooking, in a sauté pan on medium heat, sauté onions, peppers, celery, zucchini and carrots for 8 minutes.

Add these to the beans and water. Add tomatoes and paste at this time too.

Add all of the spices and taste after 30-40 minutes. We like it spicy, so I add extra jalapenos and chili powder. Simmer another 15-20 minutes. Two hours seems about right for total cooking time. It secms during the cooking process the spices are absorbed...that's why I over spice it. Serves 10-15

Lene's French Vegetable Soup

- ➤ 1/2 red onion diced
- ➤ 1 sweet potato or russet potato
- ➤ 1 cup diced broccoli with the stem
- ➤ 1 cup diced carrots
- ➤ 1/2 cup of diced turnip
- ➤ 6 cloves of garlic
- ➤ 2 cubes of vegetable bouillon
- ➤ 1 cup of diced zucchini, green or yellow
- ➤ 6 cups of water
- ➤ 1/2 tsp. of thyme
- ➤ Herbamare, sea salt or celery salt
  "to your taste"

In a soup pot, add all the ingredients and simmer in water, on low, until soft. Then use a "hand food processor" or blender to puree vegetables. Add more water depending on how thick your children like it. Add croutons to the bowl of soup and sprinkle with fresh Parmesan cheese....kids will love it.

Flu and Cold Season
Vegetable Broth

- ➤ 4 large potato peelings (only peelings)
- ➤ 5 stalks of celery cut in a few pieces
- ➤ Handful of parsley
- ➤ 10-15 cloves garlic whole
- ➤ 6 carrot peelings (only peelings)
- ➤ Handful of fresh spinach
- ➤ Handful of fresh kale and/or chard
- ➤ Handful of fresh bok choy, if available
- ➤ 4-6 tablespoons Herbamare or your favorite seasoning
- ➤ 1 jalapeno chopped (optional)
- ➤ 1 onion cut in half

In a large soup pot, add all of the above ingredients. Add just enough distilled or purified water to cover the vegetables. Cover and cook on very low for 1 1/2 hours. Don't bring it to a boil, not even a slow boil.

Strain and drink warm or cold. Vegetable broth will keep in the refrigerator, for three to four days. Vegetable broth is cleansing and has an alkalizing effect on the body and is rich with minerals. It's very healing to drink during the flu season. Always have some on hand in the freezer for those times of the flu.

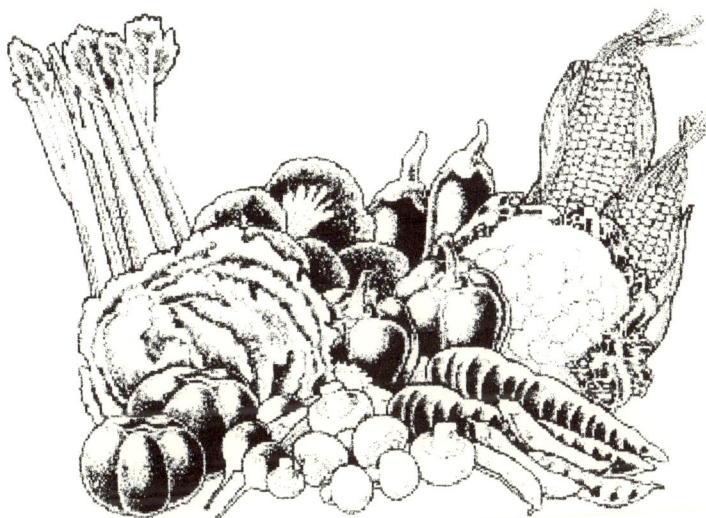

Lidle Café Specialties

Baked Turkey and
Potato Casserole Surprise

Vegetable Sandwich Spread

Seared Tomato and Cauliflower

Lene's Salmon Nuggets

Green Beans & Garlic Mashed Potatoes

Baked Turkey and
Potato Casserole Surprise

I created this dish about two and a half years ago, just before I prayed for the passion to cook. It was among the few things, to my SURPRISE that turned out. Men and children really like this recipe.

Baked Turkey

In a baking pan, place 4 stalks of celery, cut in half. Place the turkey breast with bone or without bone on top of the celery. Spread a little bit of olive oil on top of the turkey breast and sprinkle with garlic salt. Slice onions and place on top.

Cook in oven at 400F for one or more hours, depending on how large the breast is (read the instructions on turkey breast for cooking time).

Potato Casserole Surprise

- ➤ 5 potatoes peeled and cubed in bite size pieces
- ➤ 2 stalks of celery cut thin
- ➤ 1 zucchini cut thin

- Handful of cauliflower cut in bite sizes
- 1/2 red pepper chopped
- 1/2- 1 onion chopped
- 4 or more cloves of garlic chopped
- 2 or more tablespoons of Herbamare
- 1 tablespoon of Italian seasoning
- Big pinch of Paprika (optional)
- 2-4 tablespoons of olive oil (more makes a little sauce, less is probably better for your health)
- Big pinch of sweet basil or little bit of rosemary
- Jalapeno chopped (optional)

In a mixing bowl, add all of the above ingredients except olive oil. Add olive oil and mix. Pour into a baking dish and bake at 375° for one hour. After about 30 minutes, stir it up a bit.

Hint: Use lots of spices. It will taste great.

Serves 2-3

Lene's Salmon Nuggets

- 1 lb salmon fillet
- 1-2 eggs
- 3/4 cup bread crumbs
- Sea salt, pepper or Herbamare "to your taste"
- 2 tbsp. olive oil
- 1 tsp. dry parsley or 1 tbsp. diced fresh parsley

Rinse salmon in cold water, slice into nugget pieces.

Whip eggs in a separate bowl, mix bread crumbs in another bowl. Dip salmon nuggets into egg and then roll in the bread crumbs.

In frying pan, sauté nuggets in olive oil on medium heat, 3-4 minutes on each side or until golden brown.

Serve with couscous or brown rice, steamed broccoli with fresh grated Parmesan.

Vegetable Sandwich Spread

This spread is a winner. For this recipe a Champion Juicer is best. It will work in a Cuisinart, but the texture will be different.

- ➢ 1 cup raw almonds, soaked in water overnight
- ➢ 1/4 cup ground flax seeds (optional)
- ➢ 1/2 each, red and green or yellow bell pepper
- ➢ 1-2 cloves garlic
- ➢ 1/2 of a sweet potato
- ➢ 1-2 carrots
- ➢ 1 shallot or 1/4 – 1/2 of an onion
- ➢ 2-3 tablespoons of Herbamare
- ➢ 1 teaspoon coriander (optional)

Run all of the ingredients, except the flax seeds, through the juicer with the BLANK SCREEN on.

Put a small amount of nuts in first and push through, and then follow it with a piece of carrot or another vegetable. If you put too many nuts in at a time, it will clog up the juicer and cause it to overheat.

Spread on crackers or use as a sandwich spread. Refrigerate, keeps fresh for 4 days. Serves 4-6

Seared Tomato and Cauliflower
By Chef William of Phoenix

> ➤ Handful of cauliflower cut into bite sized pieces
> ➤ 2 tomatoes cored, remove the center and cut into 6 wedges
> ➤ 3 tablespoons shallots minced
> ➤ 1-2 cloves of garlic minced
> ➤ 2 teaspoons olive oil
> ➤ 2 tablespoon fresh chopped basil or oregano
> ➤ 4-6 Shakes of Chefs All Purpose Blend or Herbamare or your just some sea salt and pepper
> ➤ 1 teaspoon coriander

First, steam the cauliflower for a few minutes. If you don't have time, just cut them up into really small thin pieces so they cook faster. In a sauté pan over medium to high heat, cook tomatoes without olive oil for 2-3 minutes. Cooking tomatoes without oil caramelizes them and turns them alkaline.

Add olive oil, cauliflower, herbs and spices and cook over medium heat for 5-8 minutes. Just a minute before it's ready, add a splash of red wine (optional). Add a few raisins for the kids.

Green Beans
& Garlic Mashed Potatoes

Green Beans

- A couple of handfuls of fresh long green beans cut in half with the ends cut off
- 1/2 red pepper chopped, small pieces
- 1/2 zucchini julienne strips
- 2 cloves garlic minced
- 1 onion chopped
- A pinch of crushed red pepper
- A handful of sweet basil sprigs (stems & leaves)
- 3-4 shakes of Herbamare
- 2-3 tablespoons olive oil

In a large sauté pan over medium heat, sauté onions and garlic in olive oil for one minute. Add green beans, stir and cook on low heat for 15 minutes.

Add the zucchini, red peppers, crushed red peppers sweet basil and spices. Mix together, cover and cook over low heat for 15 more minutes.

Cover let stand for a few minutes. To cook green beans faster, steam them for 10 minutes or cook them in a little water for 10 minutes. Serves 2-3

Garlic Mashed Potatoes

Peel 3 potatoes and cut into chunks. Place in water and bring to boil. Add a little sea salt to the water. Boil for 20 minutes. While the potatoes are boiling, peel and mince 4-6 cloves of garlic and brown in a little olive oil until roasted.

After 20 minutes, drain the water off the potatoes leaving just a little. Add about 2 tablespoons of almond or rice milk. Add a little Herbamare or sea salt (a small piece of organic butter is good) and the roasted garlic and mash.

Serve the spicy green beans on top of the garlic mashed potatoes...yum! A meat eater may not even notice there's no meat.

SANDWICHES

and Wraps

Lidle Café Veggie Sandwich

Garden Salad Wrap

I Can't Believe It's Not Eggs Wrap

Mexican Rancheros Wrap

Hot Pepper Cashew Cheese Spread

"Almonnaise"

Lidle Café Veggie Sandwich

Veggie sandwiches are easy to make and great to take to work. They give you energy instead of taking it. If more people ate veggie sandwiches at lunch, they wouldn't need the extra café mocha to stay awake in the afternoon.

Hummus & Avocado Veggie Sandwich

- A few thin slices of tomato
- 1/4 avocado mashed with a fork
- 4 thin slices of cucumber
- A thin slice of onion (optional)
- A few sprouts
- Hummus to spread on the bread
- A dab of mustard
- A few sprinkles of sunflower seeds
- Ezekiel bread or Whole wheat pita

Vegetable Spread Sandwich

- Vegetable spread on bread
- A few thin slices of red or yellow pepper
- 4 thin slices of cucumber
- 1/4 avocado mashed with fork
- Mustard and almonnaise
- Leaf of Romaine lettuce
- On Ezekiel bread, cabbage or lettuce leaves

Garden Salad Wrap

This is a wonderful way to eat your salad. Your kids may even eat salad this way, because the tortilla covers up what's inside.

- 1 tomato chopped into small pieces
- 1/2 cucumber diced
- 1 avocado diced
- A little chopped onion (optional)
- 1/2 yellow or green bell pepper diced
- 5-8 lettuce leaves torn into small pieces
- A pinch of fresh basil
- Sprouts
- Hummus to spread on tortilla
- Large whole wheat or spinach tortilla

In a bowl, mix the above ingredients and spoon into a tortilla with hummus spread on it...and wrap it up.

Lidle Café Twist: Spread some CedarBrook avocado dressing on the tortilla first or dip the wrap into the dip as you eat it. Try your wrap with some hot pepper cheese spread inside. Try putting the filling in a lettuce leave and skip the tortilla. Serves 1

I Can't Believe It's Not Eggs Wrap

You won't believe it's not eggs! This wrap is delicious!

- ➤ 1 package firm organic tofu
- ➤ 1/2 - 1 onion chopped
- ➤ 1/2 of a small zucchini julienned
- ➤ 1 corn on the cob (cut kernels off)
- ➤ 1/3 of a red, green or yellow bell pepper (chopped) Mix all three for more color
- ➤ A teaspoon or more of Turmeric and a few shakes of Herbamare
- ➤ 1 clove of garlic or a few shakes of garlic powder
- ➤ A little olive oil
- ➤ Large whole wheat or spinach tortilla

Cut the kernels off the fresh corn. Don't cut too close to the core. In a medium sauté pan over medium heat with no oil, cook the corn about 3 minutes. Add onions and garlic and continue cooking for 2 minutes.

Add tofu and turmeric, mix together for 3 more minutes (mash tofu with a fork and it will look like scrambled eggs). Add the rest of the ingredients including spices for 3-4 more minutes. If you prefer vegetables more cooked add an additional 4 minutes then wrap it up!

Mexican Rancheros Wrap

- ➤ 3-4 organic eggs scrambled
- ➤ 1/2 onion chopped
- ➤ 1/2 small zucchini diced bite sizes
- ➤ 2 cloves garlic minced
- ➤ 1/2 green pepper chopped
- ➤ 1/2 jalapeno minced
- ➤ 3 or more tablespoons of salsa
- ➤ A few pinches of cilantro
- ➤ Large whole wheat or spinach tortilla

In a sauté pan over medium heat, sauté onions and garlic for 5 minutes. Add peppers, zucchini, and jalapeno. Cook 2 minutes. Stir often. Fold in the eggs and add salsa, spices and cilantro. Cook until eggs to your liking.

Wrap up the filling in a warmed sprouted or whole wheat, or spinach tortilla.

Rancheros wrap is delicious accompanied by a side of refried beans.

Serves 2

Hot Pepper Cashew Cheese Spread or Dip

- 1 cup water
- 1 cup raw cashews
- 3 tablespoons brewer's yeast
- 1 teaspoon onion powder
- Juice of 1/2 lemon
- 3-4 tablespoons fresh green chilies or
  1 small jar of green chilies
- 1/4 teaspoon sea salt
- 1/4 fresh red pepper or green pepper
- 1 jalapeno
- 1 teaspoon garlic powder or 1 clove garlic

Blend all ingredients in blender until smooth and place in refrigerator for 15 minutes. Hot pepper cheese spread is really good on sandwiches, toast, baked potato and cut up carrot and celery sticks. Will keep in refrigerator for 3 to 4 days.

Lidle Twist: Try adding fajita or taco seasoning in place of the jalapeno.

Almonnaise

I made this for the first time a few years ago and now it is a staple in my home. We use it just like mayonnaise.

- ➤ 1/2 cup blanched almonds
- ➤ 1/2 cup water or almond milk
- ➤ 1 clove garlic
- ➤ 1/2 teaspoon Herbamare or herb seasoning
- ➤ 1/2 teaspoon sea salt
- ➤ 3 tablespoons fresh lemon juice
- ➤ 1/2 - 1 cup olive oil (I don't use extra virgin in this recipe)

To blanch almonds, place almonds in boiling water for 1 minute. Strain off water and hold almonds between your fingers and squeeze. The skin just pops off. Kids love to pop the skins off.

Place almonds in the blender with water and blend for a few minutes. Add the rest of the ingredients using only one half of the oil at first. Blend for a few minutes and slowly add the remaining oil. If it's still too thick add a little more almond milk. Lidle Café Twist: Add jalapeno, cayenne pepper, fajita seasoning, and chives, even dill. Stays fresh in refrigerator for 4 – 6 days.

Rainbow Salad

CedarBrook Avocado Dressing

Potato Salad with Almonnaise

Rainbow Salad

Every color of the rainbow is in this salad. Before eating it take a minute to appreciate the colors. This salad is made without lettuce. It can keep in the refrigerator for four days. It gets better each day. Just add lettuce each day if you choose to. Make this salad once a week or every two weeks because then you don't have to chop vegetables for at least four days.

Rainbow salad takes about 30 minutes to prepare when using all of the ingredients below. It's worth the time.

In a large salad bowl add:

- 1 cucumber sliced thin and cut in two
- 1/2 orange bell pepper chopped
- 1/2 yellow bell pepper chopped
- 1/2 head of broccoli, shaved thin
- 1/2 head cauliflower, shaved thin
- 1 cup or less purple cabbage, shaved thin
- 1 small zucchini, sliced thin and quartered
- 1-2 tomatoes, quartered
- 1/2 red onion diced (optional)
- 1 clove garlic chopped or pressed
- 1 apple with skin on cut thin, small pieces
- 1/2 cup pecans or walnuts or both

- ➤ A small handful of fresh sweet basil chopped
  or 1 tablespoon dried basil
- ➤ A few big shakes of Herbamare
- ➤ A few big pinches of fresh or dried oregano
  or a few big pinches of Italian seasoning
- ➤ Olive oil about 4-6 tablespoons or more to your taste
- ➤ Juice of 1/2 lemon or ½ lime (optional)
- ➤ 2-4 tablespoons Balsamic vinegar
- ➤ 4-8 tablespoons of Annie's Tuscany Dressing (If you can't get Annie's Tuscany, use an Italian dressing)

Mix all the ingredients together and let it sit a few minutes before serving. Add romaine lettuce, as you need it. Lettuce will get soggy in the refrigerator.

When eating this salad the next day, let is sit out for 10 minutes. It's better when it's not so cold. How to use Rainbow Salad:

1. Great in pita pockets with hummus spread inside.
2. Put some into a tortilla with lettuce and wrap it up.
3. Cook up some corn quinoa clbow pasta or soy penne pasta, let cool and mix into salad to make pasta salad.

CedarBrook
Avocado Dressing or Dip

Put 1 cup of water in blender and add:
- 3/4 cups raw cashews

Add 1 more cup of water and add:
- 1/4 cup raw sesame seeds
- 1/2 avocado
- 1-2 cloves garlic
- Pinch of cayenne
- 1 teaspoon sea salt
- 1 teaspoon onion powder
- Juice of one lemon

Blend all ingredients 1-2 minutes, until smooth.

The Lidle Café Twist: Add 1/2 cucumber and sweet basil or add green pepper and jalapeno. If you don't have sesame seeds or cashews, raw almonds work really well. Try doing the recipe with almond milk. Add dill or any other of your favorite herbs. If limes are juicy, squeeze some juice into the mixture. Add less water to make avocado dip.

Potato Salad with Almonnaise

This potato salad is better than potato salad made with mayonnaise. It's simply delicious.

- ➤ 1 full recipe of Almonnaise
- ➤ 10 medium, diced cooked potatoes (boil 20 min.)
- ➤ 1/4 cup celery chopped
- ➤ 1/4 cup drained olives chopped
- ➤ 1/2 red onion chopped
- ➤ 1 tablespoon Celtic sea salt
- ➤ 2 cloves garlic pressed
- ➤ 1 teaspoon dill
- ➤ 1/3 cup green pepper chopped
- ➤ 1 teaspoon Herbamare with a pinch of cayenne pepper
- ➤ 3-5 radishes thinly sliced
- ➤ Add turmeric 1/4 teaspoon at a time to get desired color

For a zesty flavor add a little mustard sauce. For a sweeter flavor add a little Honey.

Put all ingredients in a bowl and mix well. If it looks too dry add more Almonnaise.

ITALIAN

Lene's Vegetable & Meatball Marinara

Vegetable Pasta Primavera

Pistachio Pesto Pasta

Lene's
Vegetable & Meatball Marinara

This is a very clever way to get kids to eat their vegetables. The vegetables are mixed in with the meatballs. Try it and see for yourself.

1) Meat portion of the meatball

- 2 lbs of turkey, buffalo or ground meat
- 2 medium sized eggs lightly mixed with fork
- 1 cup of bread crumbs
- 1/4 cup of dried parsley or 3/4 cup of fresh chopped parsley
- 1/2 cup of grated Parmesan
- 2 cloves garlic, minced or crushed

2) Vegetable portion of the meatball

- 1 sweet potato, small cubed
- 1 1/2 cups of diced broccoli
- 1/2 cup of diced carrots
- 3 cups baby spinach (regular okay)
- 1/4 diced onion (or red is sweeter)
- 4 cloves of garlic, minced or crushed
- 16 oz water

3) Tomato marinara sauce

- ➢ 3 tbsp. Olive oil, extra virgin
- ➢ 2 cloves of garlic, crushed
- ➢ 1/2 of a carrot, grated
- ➢ 2 – 12oz cans of crushed or diced tomatoes
- ➢ 1 – 6oz can of tomato paste
- ➢ 10 – 14 leaves fresh basil (dried is ok)
- ➢ Sea salt and pepper to taste
- ➢ 2 – 4 tbsp. of honey
- ➢ 1/2 of a lemon

STEP 1
Cook the vegetable portion #2 in the 16oz of slow boiling water for 25 minutes or until soft. Drain water and SAVE for broth, later in the preparation.

Place cooked vegetables in a blender or food processor and puree.

STEP 2
Set oven to 400F
Spread olive oil lightly on cookie sheet – tray

STEP 3

In a large bowl add the meat portion #1 and the vegetable portion #2.

Mix together with a tablespoon and form into round meatballs. Then roll them lightly in bread crumbs and place on cookie sheet.

You can make 26 –30 meatballs, depending on size. Cook vegetable meatballs for 8 – 10 minutes each side. While cooking meatballs prepare marinara sauce.

STEP 4

Marinara sauce – In a large pot (big enough for all the meatballs and sauce) sauté crushed garlic and grated carrot in oil for 2-3 minutes.

Then, add the crushed tomatoes and tomato paste to the pot with the sautéed garlic and carrot.

Add 12oz of water and the fresh basil leaves (or dried). Stir and puree the sauce with the hand food processor, mixer or place all of it in a blender and blend.

Add 2 tablespoons of honey. Cut the lemon in half and squeeze the juices into the marinara sauce.

STEP 5

When the meatballs are finished, place them into marinara sauce and allow to cook on low heat, for at least one hour.

The longer they cook the better the meatballs and the sauce will be. Stir occasionally and add water if the sauce seems too thick.

This will be good for three days in the refrigerator or freeze for future use.

Vegetable Pasta Primavera

- ➤ 1 small zucchini, diced
- ➤ 2-4 cloves garlic minced or crushed
- ➤ 1/2 cup cauliflower, sliced thin (shaved)
- ➤ 1/4 to 1/2 cup broccoli, (shaved)
- ➤ 1/4 red onion, chopped (optional)
- ➤ 1-2 tablespoons olive oil
- ➤ 1 or 2 jars of marinara sauce (check label) 1 jar will make thick sauce, 2 jars for thinner sauce
- ➤ 6-8 Brussels sprouts for meatballs (optional)
- ➤ 1 tablespoon dried Italian seasoning

In a medium saucepan, sauté the garlic and onions in olive oil for 8 minutes.

If add Brussels sprouts, begin to steam them before you begin to sauté the garlic and onions. Steam them for 15 - 20 minutes.

After 8 minutes, add zucchini, cauliflower and broccoli and sauté for 10 minutes. Add marinara sauce and spices. If you add Brussels sprouts, cut each Brussels sprout in half and stir into sauce. Top with grated Parmesan. Let cook on low heat for 10 minutes. Serve over corn quinoa, soy, brown rice spaghetti or brown rice angel hair pasta. Serves 3-5

Pistachio Pesto Pasta

> - 3/4 cup raw pistachios
> - 2 or more cloves of garlic
> - Small handful of fresh basil
> - A few big pinches of fresh oregano or a big pinch of dried oregano
> - A big pinch of fresh parsley or dried
> - Olive oil (I don't use Extra Virgin Olive oil in this recipe because the taste is too strong, it may be fine for you)
> - 1 –2 tablespoons of dried Italian seasoning if you don't have any fresh herbs
> - 2 tablespoons of dried pesto seasoning if you don't have any other herbs
> - 16 oz of corn quinoa elbow pasta or soy penne pasta

Grind the pistachios in a food processor until the mix is coarse but fine (not powder). Empty into the bowl you are going to use to serve the pasta in. Place the fresh herbs and garlic into the processor and chop. Add to the pistachios.

Add the rest of the herbs and mix. Pour enough olive oil to this mixture so it's kind of creamy, with a little olive oil showing in the pesto.

If it clumps together it's too dry.   Start with about 5 tablespoons of olive oil. You should be able to see some of the oil in the pesto mixture.

We use 16 oz of corn quinoa elbow pasta. Don't over cook the pasta; it should be a little firm when finished. Angel hair pasta doesn't work well.   Soy penne pasta is good too.   Shorter pastas work best.

Serve as soon as you mix the pasta into the pesto, it gets cold quickly. Grate a little Parmesan and sprinkle on top.   (use less garlic if your kids don't like garlic or leave out of recipe) Serves 2-3

Lidle Café
Sunday Brunch Special

Tortilla Española

Tortilla Española

This is a tradition and staple breakfast for many of the local residents of Spain. They serve it at room temperature (I prefer it hot).

- 2 large russet or 3 white potatoes
- 5 eggs
- 1/2 -1 onion chopped
- 1-3 cloves garlic minced
- Olive oil
- 1-2 tablespoons Herbamare or your favorite seasoning or some sea salt

Peel and cut the potatoes into small pieces. Boil in water for 20 minutes and drain. In a large sauté pan on medium heat, sauté onions and garlic for 8 minutes. While garlic and onions are cooking, scramble the eggs and add the spices.

Crush up the potatoes a bit with a fork so there is still some small pieces, but most of it is kind of mashed up. Add potatoes to the onions and garlic and mix...then add the eggs.

Let it cook for a few minutes...after about 2 minutes use a spatula to separate some of the inside so the uncooked egg can get closer to the bottom of the pan and cook a little. After about 3-4 minutes use the spatula to loosen up the bottom of the mixture. At this point it should look 75% done and somewhat formed.

Remove the pan from the stove and place a plate over the top of the pan...FLIP it upside down holding the plate firmly in place under the pan...shake the pan a bit to loosen the Tortilla Española.

Once it comes out onto the plate, slide it back into the pan and continue to cook for 3-5 more minutes. It may turn out a little dry your first time or it may turn out perfect. If it falls apart a bit, just reform it in the pan...it will remold itself instantly.

If, when you flip it onto the plate and the pan looks too dry, just add a bit of olive oil to the pan and let it heat up before returning the Tortilla Española back in.

When it is finished it will look like a round cake mold. Slide it onto a plate and let it stand a minute to firm up. Cut into wedges and serve warm or hot. At the Lidle Café, we serve it with Ezekiel Toast and Fresh Fruit.

Lidle Café Twist: To spice it up add: chopped green chili's, jalapeno, fajita or taco spice.
Serves 3-4

Desserts You Can Eat Anytime!

Smart Smoothies

Zesty Lemon Pudding

Delicious No-Bake Apple Pie

Orange-Date Dessert Bars

Fruit Fondue

Energy Candy

Smart Smoothies

Smoothies are quick and easy to make. All you need is a blender and a base of fresh or frozen fruit. The best fruits to have on hand (in the freezer) are: Strawberries, bananas, mangos, blueberries, pineapple, raspberries and peaches.

Blend smoothies for a minute or two.

Strawberry Banana Smoothie

- 1 cup apple juice
- 1 handful of strawberries
- 1 banana
- 1 tablespoon flaxseed oil
- A little plain yogurt (optional)
- A few dates (optional)

Very Berry Smoothie

- 1/2 cup strawberries
- 1/2 cup raspberries
- 1/4 cup blueberries
- 1 banana
- 1 cup almond, soy or rice milk
- 1-2 tablespoons flaxseed oil
- A few dates (optional)
- 1/2 cup ice (optional)

Tropical Smoothie

- ➤ 1 cup almond, soy or rice milk
- ➤ 1 cup mango's
- ➤ 1/2 cup pineapple chunks
- ➤ 1/4 – 1/2 shredded coconut
- ➤ 1 tablespoon flaxseed oil
- ➤ A little plain yogurt (optional)

Brain Smoothie

- ➤ 1 cup apple juice or pineapple juice
- ➤ 1 banana
- ➤ ½ cup pineapple chunks
- ➤ 1 scoop Vita Pro
- ➤ 1-2 tablespoon flaxseed oil
- ➤ ½ cup water

- • See resource page for "Vita Pro" – vitamin and protein nutrition drink

Zesty Lemon Pudding

Once you get past the few contemplative bites you will agree this pudding is good...really good. The texture is hearty, yet creamy.

- 1 cup raw cashews pre-soaked 8 hours
- 6 dates pre-soaked 8 hours, pitted and cut into small pieces
- 1 lemon, peeled, seeded and cut into chunks
- Juice of 1 lemon
- 1 tablespoon flaxseed oil
- Maple syrup
- Almond milk

In a blender, combine cashews and lemon juice. Blend until smooth. Add lemon pieces, dates and flaxseed oil. Blend until smooth. Taste and if it tastes too tart, add a little maple syrup. If it's not tart enough, add more lemon and lemon juice. If it is too thick, add a little almond milk.

Lidle Café Twist: Melt a handful of carob chips and swirl on top of pudding with some fresh raspberries. Eat within 4 hours. Serves 3-5

Delicious No-Bake Apple Pie

CRUST

- 1/2 cup dried un-sulfured apricots, pre-soak in water at least 4 hours
- 2 cups raw almonds
- 3 tablespoons ground flaxseed (optional, highly recommended
- 1/4 cup of raisins, pre-soaked in water, for 1 -2 hours
- A few big pinches of unsweetened coconut (optional)
- A big pinch of grated lemon peel

Blend in food processor, work into dough and press into pie plate or two.

FILLING

- 8-10 apples (Granny Smith are good)
- 3/4 cup raisins, pre-soak in water 4 hours
- 1/4- 1/2 cup fresh apricots or dried apricots, pre-soaked for 4 hours
- 2-4 teaspoons cinnamon
- 1/2 -1 teaspoon allspice
- A few shakes of coriander
- A few pinches of grated lemon peel

Core and chop apples into bite size pieces. You can peel the apples or leave the peel on.

Take half the apples and the rest of the ingredients and spices, including a few teaspoons of water from the raisins, and mix in food processor. Applesauce consistency or a little chunkier is good.

Set aside and mix the rest of the apples in food processor leaving some chunks for texture. Mix together with the first batch and pour into pie shells.

Lidle Café Twist: Substitute raw pistachios for the almonds. You can use more or less apples...eliminate the apricots if you choose...try fresh peaches and apples. Create your own signature apple pie.

Orange-Date Dessert Bars

This is a very easy dessert to prepare. These bars are great to take to work, and give your kids for lunch, or breakfast or after dinner. This is one of my favorite recipes from The Raw Gourmet. It is a great foundation recipe to add your own twists to.

CRUST

> ➤ 2 cups raw almonds, pecans or walnuts (or try a mixture of all three and a little pistachio nut)
> ➤ 1 cup oat flour
> ➤ A pinch of coriander
> ➤ 4 tablespoons maple syrup

FILLING

> ➤ 2 cups pitted dates, pre-soak 30-60 minutes
> ➤ 3 tablespoons water
> ➤ Juice and zest (grated rind) of a large orange

Juice the orange and soak the dates in the juice and water.

For crust: Place nuts in food processor and mix until coarsely ground. Add oat flour and pulse to mix. Add coriander and syrup, one tablespoon at a time until mixture holds together.

Press 1/2 of the crust into a lightly oiled pan.

For the filling: In the food processor, combine the dates, the water they soaked in, and orange zest. Puree until smooth.

Spread the date mixture over the crust. Crumble the remaining crust over the top. Press the top crumble lightly into the filling and smooth out the best you can.

*To make oat flour, place whole, raw oat berries or oat grouts in an electric seed grinder. Grind to make flour, and sift any hard bits.

Lidle Café Twist: Fold in fresh raspberries or strawberries into the filling. Add pre-soaked dried apricots, cranberries and blueberries to the filling. Add carob chips to the crust and a little coconut. Serves 6-10

Fruit Fondue

Fruit Fondue is a fast, easy and fun treat. Kids love it. It may be a way to get them to eat more fruit. If your kids say "Yuk" to carob chips, tell them they are chocolate chips. Or better yet, don't even tell them until after they have eaten them.

> ➤ 1 banana, sliced in 1/4 inch pieces
> ➤ 10 strawberries, left whole
> ➤ 1 apple, cut into wedges
> ➤ 1 orange, separate slices
> ➤ 1 or more cups melted carob chips
>   or organic chocolate

Melt the carob chips in a fondue pot or in a small saucepan on top of the stove on low heat. Pour the sauce into a dipping bowl and watch excitement begin.

Put some ground flaxseeds, chopped nuts, unsweetened shredded coconut and some chocolate sprinkles (for a weekend treat) into a few bowls and dip the fruit fondue into them.

Energy Candy

Another recipe your kids will like. Energy candy is great to take to school and to work.

Energy Candy can be made with or without nuts.

- ➤ 1/3 cup dates
- ➤ 1/3 cup raisins
- ➤ 1/3 cup dried cranberries
- ➤ 1/4 cup raw sunflower seeds
- ➤ 1/4 cup raw pumpkin seeds
- ➤ 1/4 cup raw almonds
- ➤ 1/4 cup raw cashews
- ➤ 1/4 cup un-sulfured dried apricots
- ➤ 3-4 prunes (optional)
- ➤ 3 tablespoons ground flaxseed
- ➤ 1/2 cup unsweetened coconut

Place all of the above ingredients in a food processor and mix. Form into small balls. Save some of the above coconut and roll the balls in the coconut or in carob powder.

RESOURCES

Books

Excitotoxins,
The Taste that Kills, by
Russell L. Blaylock, M.D.

Talking Back To Ritalin
by Peter R. Breggin, M.D.

A Consumer's Dictionary
of Food Additives
by Ruth Winter, M.S.

The PDR, Pocket Guide to
Prescription Drugs

Triumph Over Cancer, A
Natural Approach
by Agi Lidle, Herbalist

Prescription for Nutritional
Healing by
James F. Balch, M.D.,
Phyllis A. Balch, C.N.C.

The Prayer of Jabez
by Bruce Wilkinson

The Essential Guide to
Prescription Drugs 2002
By James J. Rybachki,
Pharm. D.

Websites

www.abetterlife.info
www.askdrsears.com
www.PDR.net
www.webMD.com

VitaPro Nutrition Drink
www.abetterlife.info

Well Being Health Center
BioSET Allergy Testing
Dr. Kyle D. Christensen
6024 San Juan Ave Suite B
Citrus Heights, CA 95610
916-725-7533

Nancy Harkins,
International Speaker
602-749-9055
nancyharkins@earthlink.net

Tourette Syndrome Assn.
Inc. 1-888-486-8738

Attention Deficit Disorder
Assn. 1-847-432-ADDA

Mountain Peoples Warehouse
1-800-679-8735

School of Natural Healing
Natural Health Courses
1-800-372-8255

Bibliography

Russell L. Blaylock, M.D., **Excitotoxins, The Taste that Kills**, Health Press, Santa Fe, New Mexico, 1997.

Peter R. Breggin, M.D., **Talking Back to Ritalin, What Doctors aren't telling you about stimulants for children**, Common Courage Press, Monroe, ME 1998.

Jethro Kloss, **Back to Eden**, Back to Eden Books Publishing Company, Loma Linda, California, 1997.

Ruth Winter, M.S., **A Consumer's Dictionary of Food Additives**, Three Rivers Press / New York, 1994.

N.W. Walker, D.Sc., **Become Younger**, Norwalk Press, Prescott, AZ, 1995.

Nancy Appleton, PhD, **Lick The Sugar Habit**, Avery Publishing Group, New York, 1996.

Bruce Wilkinson, **The Prayer of Jabez**, Multnomah Publishers, Inc., Sisters, Oregon, 2000.

Agi Lidle, **Triumph Over Cancer, A Natural Approach**, A Better Life Publishing, Scottsdale, Arizona, 2001

Website Resources

www.askdrsears.com • www.PDR.net • www.webMD.com
www.healthdoc.com • www.bbll.com

Newspaper Article – "You really do need multivitamins, AMA says" by Ronald Kotulak, Chicago Tribune – 6/19/02

About the Author

Agi Lidle is a breast cancer survivor, herbalist, author and business owner, who is dedicated to providing people with the best information available on natural health and healing. She is a graduate of The John R. Christopher, School of Natural Healing.

"Triumph Over ADD, ADHD & Tourette Syndrome" is the second book in her "Triumph Over" book series. The first book "Triumph Over Cancer, A Natural Approach" details her victory over cancer using completely natural methods.

Agi teaches a course on ADD, ADHD & Tourette syndrome at the Harkins Wellness Center in Scottsdale, Arizona. She also teaches cooking classes detailing the healthy food program outlined in her book, while demonstrating recipes from the Lidle Café cookbook.

As a recognized inspirational speaker, educator and facilitator, Agi delivers her message of hope to schools, groups and businesses across the country.

To contact Agi personally, email her at:

ablhealth@aol.com

online at: www.abetterlife.info

First book in the "Triumph Over" Series

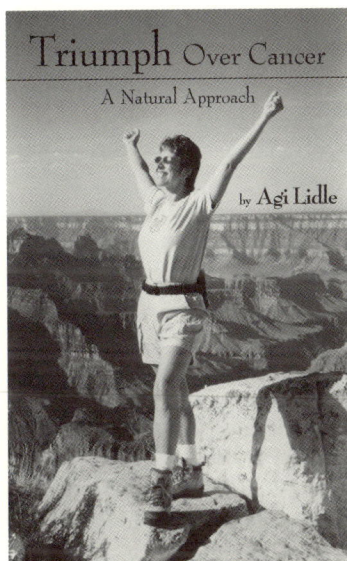

ISBN 0-9671693-1-3

★★★★★ **A "can-do" emotional and physical motivator"**

Reviewer: Midwest Book Review, Oregon, WI USA, July 8, 2002

"From adopting a healthy diet, to maintaining a positive attitude, Triumph Over Cancer is a "can-do" emotional and physical motivator with lifestyle advice valid for everyone of any age or background, and whether they have a current diagnosis, or family history of cancer, or simply want to be as healthy and fit as they can be despite any health handicap or obstacle."